Ethical Issues in Anthropological Research

About the Editor

Subir Biswas (b.1974) teaches Anthropology at the West Bengal State University since 2009 as Associate Professor. Before that he worked for North Bengal University as Assistant Professor since 2001. He obtained his Master degree in Anthropology from Calcutta University in 1996 and Ph. D. (2010) from North Bengal University. In course of his association with N.B.U., he has experienced with several fieldworks within the range of Northern part of West Bengal. His areas of interests are Anthropological Demography, Health and Bioethics. He has in his credit several research projects of UGC, ICSSR, CWS (NBU), associateship of IIAS as well as several research articles of Anthropological interests published in national and international journals. He is also member of several professional Anthropological associations/governmental bodies.

Ethical Issues in Anthropological Research

Edited by
Subir Biswas

CONCEPT PUBLISHING COMPANY PVT. LTD.
NEW DELHI-110059

ISBN-13 : 978-93-5125-090-6

First Published 2014

Published and Printed by

Concept Since 1974

Concept Publishing Company Pvt. Ltd.
A/15-16, Commercial Block, Mohan Garden
New Delhi-110059 (India)
T: 25351460, 25351794, *F*: 091-11-25357109
E: publishing@conceptpub.com, W: www.conceptpub.com
Editorial Office: H-13, Bali Nagar, New Delhi-110 015, India.

Cataloging in Publication Data—*Courtesy:* D.K. Agencies (P) Ltd. <docinfo@dkagencies.com>

"Ethical Issues in Anthropological Research" (Seminar) (2012 : West Bengal State University)
Ethical issues in anthropological research / edited by Subir Biswas.
p. cm.
Includes bibliographical references and index.
ISBN 9789351250906

1. Anthropology—Research—Congresses. 2. Anthropology—Moral and ethical aspects--Congresses. 3. Anthropology—Fieldwork—Moral and ethical aspects—Congresses. I. Biswas, Subir, 1974- II. Title.

DDC 174.9301 23

Preface

I

Anthropology is a multidisciplinary field of science, which includes the study of all aspects of humankind—archaeological, biological, linguistic and socio-cultural. Anthropology has roots in the natural and social sciences and in the humanities, ranging in approach from basic to applied research. Ethics is concerned with the conduct of human beings. Ethics does not prescribe a specific set of rules or policies. Instead, it provides a framework for evaluating problems and determining an appropriate course of action. Ethical analysis should reflect both internationally accepted norms and locally relevant cultural values.

Anthropologists criticize some components of bioethics because of their abstract principles derived from arm-chair philosophy and lack of cross-cultural analysis (and ethnocentric view) for that they prepare a readymade ethical code of conduct which may differ significantly from culture to culture. Therefore, this volume aims to investigate such area of bioethics which may criticize in the light of anthropological fieldwork. The work also finds some area of bioethics to study cultural construct of morality including cross-cultural analysis keeping in mind cultural relativism in true sense.

The title of this volume, "Ethical Issues in Anthropological Research" is significant in light of the fact that ethics is prerequisite for the protection of participants under study. The international community has repeatedly acknowledged the importance of ethics in research among human participants. For instance, as per American Anthropological Association code of ethics (1998) "Anthropologists have a duty to be informed about ethical codes relating to their work, and ought periodically to receive training on current research activities and ethical issues. In addition, departments offering anthropology degrees should include and require ethical training in their curriculums".

II

The present work is an outcome of national seminar entitled "Ethical Issues in Anthropological Research" organized by Department of Anthropology, West Bengal State University during 19-20 January, 2012. Keeping in mind the importance and application of the topic, ten selected papers are being included in this volume.

In the first chapter, Prof. A.K. Kapoor in his article "Ethical Issues and Perspectives" examines historical dimensions of ethical issues; identify issues, perspectives and explain potential benefit specially in respect of anthropological research. Prof. Rajatsubhra Mukhopadhyay in his article "Ethics in Social Research: Issues in Perspective" describes ethical issues in social sciences specially in respect of anthropology and sociological studies in India. The title of the paper by Dr Som Prasad Khatiwada indicates that he make an effort to point out "Ethical Issues in Ethno-archaeological Research". Dr Vijay Prakash Sharma in his article "Ethics and Anthropological fieldwork: Problems and Consequences" report his findings on ethics as a part of Applied and Action Anthropology intervention programme. Dr A.S. Arunkumar and Dr Jesurathan Deverapalli in their paper "Paying Informants in

Ethnographic Research: Issues of Ethics and Quality" examine the impact of payment in field research. Dr Shyamal Kumar Nandy in his article "Fieldwork for Anthropological Research: Some Ethical Issues" reviews ethical issues of anthropological fieldwork with examples from his own field experience. Dr Samar Kumar Biswas in his article "Ethical Issues of Anthropology with Special Reference to Fieldwork" also examines ethical issues in anthropological research from his own field experiences. Ms Madhurima Chowdhury in her paper "Global Ethic, Rights and Responsibility" examines rights and responsibility in respect of global ethics and also pointed out basic principles of human rights. Mr Ashok Das Gupta in his article "Ethical Issues in Research on Social-Cultural Anthropology" examines ethical issues specially code of ethics of American Anthropological association. Dr S. Yaseen Saheb and others in their article "Ethical Issues in Epidemiological Study of Type 2 Diabetes among the Gangadikara Vokkaliga of Karnataka State" highlighted ethical issues encountered and compliance for the said research.

III

The seminar was sponsored by Indian Council of Social Science Research, Eastern Regional Centre, Kolkata. It was possible to organize successfully only through the active participation of students, and scholars of Department of Anthropology, West Bengal State University. I am grateful to my colleagues Dr Abhijit Das and Mr Debasis Kumar Mondal for valuable help and co-operation. I am also grateful to Prof Ashoke Ranjan Thakur, the then Vice-Chancellor of the University for financial support, kind permission and guidance to arrange the seminar. I am thankful to all the delegates from various parts of the country for their active participation. Last but not the least; I want to express my thanks to my wife, Dr Gargi Biswas (Saha) for cooperation and support during seminar days.

Hope this worl. will be of interest not only to anthropologists or scholars of related field but also funding agencies and participant/ beneficiaries of the said field.

Subir Biswas

Contents

List of Contributors

A.K. Kapoor (Prof.), Former Vice-Chancellor, Jiwaji University and Professor, Department of Anthropology, Delhi University, Delhi-110007, Email: anupkapoor46@rediffmail.com

A.S. Arunkumar (Dr.), Research Scholar, Department of Anthropology, Pondicherry University, Puducherry-605014, Email: akred04@gmail.com

Ashok Das Gupta, UGC-JRF, Department of Anthropology, North Bengal University, RajaRammohunpur, Dist-Darjeeling, West Bengal-734013, Email: marhabah35@gmail.com

B.N. Sarkar (Dr.), Anthropologist (Physical), Anthropological Survey of India, 27, Jawaharlal Nehru Road, Kolkata-700016 Email: drbnsarkar@yahoo.com

B.V. Ravi Prasad (Dr.), Research Associate (Physical), Anthropological Survey of India, Manav Bhavan, Bogadi 2nd Stage, Mysore Karnataka State, India, Email: venkata.raviprasad@gmail.com

D. Lokanath, Junior Research Fellow, Anthropological Survey of India, Manav Bhavan, Bogadi 2nd Stage, Mysore, Karnataka State, India

D. Ravindranath (Dr.), Scientist, Texas Biomedical Research Institute, San Antonio, USA.

D. Xaviour (Dr.), Research Associate (Physical), Anthropological Survey of India, Manav Bhavan, Bogadi 2nd Stage, Mysore, Karnataka State, India

H. Basavana Gowdappa (Prof.), Professor of Medicine and Principal, JSS Medical College, Mysore, Karnataka State, India

Jesurathan Deverapalli (Dr.), Assistant Professor, Department of Anthropology, Pondicherry University, Puducherry-605014
Email: drjesudev@gmail.com

K. Raghothama Rao (Prof.), Ex-Principal, JSS Medical College, Mysore, Karnataka State, India

M.A. Shekar (Dr.), Director, Apoorva Diabetes Foundation, Mysore, Karnataka State, India

Madhurima Chowdhury (Ms.), Senior research fellow, Human rights, Calcutta University, 35 Ballygunj Circular Road, Kolkata-700019, Email: chowdhury.madhurima@gmail.com

Md. Salman, Senior Research Fellow, Anthropological Survey of India, Manav Bhavan, Bogadi 2nd Stage, Mysore, Karnataka State, India

P.B.S.V. Padmanabham (Dr.), Superintendent Anthropologist (Physical), Anthropological Survey of India, 27 Jawaharlal Nehru Road, Kolkata-700016

Rajatsubhra Mukhopadhyay (Prof.), Professor, Department of Sociology, North Bengal University, RajaRammohunpur, Dist-Darjeeling, West Bengal-734013, Email: rajatsocio@rediffmail.com

S. Dasgupta, Senior Research Fellow, Anthropological Survey of India, Manav Bhavan, Bogadi 2nd Stage, Mysore, Karnataka State, India

S. Samanta (Ms.), Project Scientist, Anthropological Survey of India, Manav Bhavan, Bogadi 2nd Stage, Mysore, Karnataka State, India
Email: suprabhasamanta@yahoo.in

S. Yaseen Saheb (Dr.), Ex-Superintendent Anthropologist (Physical), Anthropological Survey of India, Manav Bhavan, Bogadi 2nd Stage, Mysore, Karnataka State, India

Samar Kumar Biswas (Dr.), Assistant Professor, Department of Anthropology, North Bengal University, RajaRammohunpur, Dist-Darjeeling, West Bengal-734013, Email: smrkbis@yahoo.co.in

Shyamal Kumar Nandy (Dr.), Research Associate (Cultural), Anthropological Survey of India (ERC), Salt Lake, Kolkata
Email: shymlnandy@yahoo.com

Som Prasad Khatiwada (Dr.), Associate Professor in NeHCA, Kirtipur Campus, Tribhuvan Univeristy, Nepal, Email: khatiwadasom@yahoo.co.in

Vijay Prakash Sharma (Dr.), Director, VAIDYAS–India, 1D, LAXMAN, Sitakunj Apartment, Professor's Colony, Karamtoli, Ranchi-834008, Jharkhand. Email: vsharma@intrahealth.org

CHAPTER 1

Ethical Issues and Perspectives

A.K. KAPOOR

Introduction

Ethics are norms for conduct that distinguish between acceptable and unacceptable behaviour. Ethics is not limited to specific acts and defined moral codes, but encompasses the whole of moral ideals and behaviours, a person's philosophy of life. Personal ethics signify a moral code applicable to individuals, while ethics mean moral theory applied to groups. Social ethics can be synonymous with social and political philosophy; inasmuch as it is the foundation of the model or ideal society or state.

Ethics and morals are respectively akin to theory and practice. Ethics denotes the theory of right and wrong actions, while morals indicate their practice within the guidelines. Ethics is concerned with the conduct of human beings. All scientific activities, including those of the social scientists, are conducted with the participation of human beings or have an impact on human beings or on the wider society and the environment. Therefore, it is essential that scientists or researchers understand ethical issues and the implications of their scientific work on society and act accordingly. In making ethical judgment, they rely upon various standards of ethics, which could be universal or specific to the culture(s) or localities. Indeed, it is essential that researchers share and discuss the ethical issues in their work and evolve collective standards of their own. But this situation may not be applicable to all societies or cultures.

When most of the people think of ethics (or morals), they think of rules for distinguishing between right and wrong. In general, people learn ethical norms at home, at school, in church, or in other social settings. Although most people acquire their sense of right and wrong during childhood, moral development occurs throughout life and human beings pass through different stages of growth as they mature. Ethical norms are so ubiquitous that one might be tempted to regard them as simple common sense. On the other hand, if morality were nothing more than common sense, then why are there so many ethical disputes and issues in our society? (Samantaray and Sahu, 2008).

One plausible explanation of these disagreements is that people recognize some common ethical norms, but many individuals interpret, apply, and balance these norms in different ways in light of their own values and life experiences. Most societies also have legal rules that govern behaviour, but ethical norms tend to be broader and more informal than laws. Although most societies use laws to enforce widely accepted moral standards and ethical and legal rules use similar concepts, it is important to remember that ethics and law are not the same. An action may be legal but unethical or illegal, but ethical (Samantaray and Sahu, 2008).

Historical Dimension of Ethical Issues

In early 1960s, U.S. Govt. suggested the social science research in foreign countries. It was alleged that the Department of Defense and other governmental institutions were using anthropologists to gather data and keep them in their insurgency and counterinsurgency activities. The most notorious instance was project Camelot in Chile, where the army had a contract with the

American university to study socio-political factors that could lead to internal warfare in that country. It was believed, that the army was directly or indirectly funding social science research and the result to be used for their purposes. It has been observed because of project Camelot, and later conflicts (especially the Vietnam War), it was widely believed that various U.S. government agencies (such as the Department of Defense, the Department of State, and the CIA) had large-scale involvement in contracting with universities, private agencies, and probably individual anthropologists, in order to gather mission-oriented intelligence data under the guise of legitimate anthropological research. The fear was that anthropologist were, witting or unwitting, serving as spies for the United States and other so-called friendly governments. Questions were raised concerning the ethics of this, especially given that the results were believed to be secret and not subject to free publication (Beals, 1967).

Government funding of all social science research became suspect: these activities were seen as posing a threat to the integrity of the universities sponsoring social research in the social sciences themselves to the individuals allegedly involved in the research (Beals, 1967). The major fears of such anthropology were twofold: (1) that anthropology's resultant bad reputation would close off future field opportunities abroad, and (2) that the information being gathered would be used by our government or others to control, enslave, and even annihilate many of the 'third world' communities that were being studied. This was the era of the Vietnam War, and it is well known that such atrocities were in fact taking place.

These types of problems surfaced among the people in the USA and they started talking about the "ethical issues'. Some of the American anthropologists also raised the "ethical issues'. Ethical issues which were raised such as the relationship between anthropologists and their informants, protection of human subjects, informed consent, anonymity of informants and communities, payment of informants, exploitation of informants and the failure to foresee the repercussions of one's research on the people being studied.

In early 1990s, a research paper was published in international journal of genetics by four American scientists on Indian data. The blood samples were collected from rural and urban areas of Tamil Nadu and there was no mention of any Indian author or any name in the acknowledgements. By chance this paper came in contact with a senior Deputy Director, Indian Council of Medical Research, New Delhi. This dynamic lady probed further and came to know very interesting facts about the publication of papers. The senior scientist of ICMR took the interest on 'ethical issues' and under her initiative first time ICMR released the ethical guidelines for the scientists in India (ICMR, 1997). Then it was followed by DBT and DST, New Delhi. It has been observed that some of the institutes are not following the ICMR guidelines. Why this dilemma and gap?

Ethical issues are just like a coin. Both sides have different meaning. On one side it is human understanding, feeling, concerns and research position and other side is requirements, legality, and research negativism and exploitation of research. Choosing one we have to keep in mind inter-, intra-, multi- and trans-disciplinary approaches for the welfare of the people/communities/ethnic groups/ population group.

Each discipline has to decide the side of the coin when we talk about discipline straight comes to the university level. Each discipline who is dealing with humans/animals/other species, the university should have their guidelines. As human scientists, we have to identify the boundaries of understanding between the minds of the people, the outcome of research, mind of the researcher and attitude towards research.

We should have a proper planning for the students, researchers and teachers for ethical consideration and it should be made as an integral part of anthropological methods. Each discipline has an association and society and these academic bodies should bring out a broad framework on ethical issues in India. Other than the anthropologists who are using anthropological methods, ethical guidelines have to be made for them also.

Issues and Perspectives

It is important to take seriously this concern about the mistreatment of human participants in research and, on the other, to keep it in correct perspective. An infamous historical event, that is, the so-called medical experiments carried out by Nazi German physicians in the concentration camps during World War-II, sensitized the world to the general problem and gave rise to the Nuremberg code of medical ethics for human experimentation. The concern aroused by these medical "experiments" has been renewed by the wide publicity given to more recent experiments in which patients have suffered damage in the course of well-intentioned efforts to try out new drugs or new surgical procedures.

While it is such developments in the medical sciences that have fueled the movement to protect research participants, the ethical in social research are no less real. They arise inevitably from the kinds of questions meaningful answers. They may be evoked by the research topic itself, the nature of the setting in which the research is conducted, the kinds of persons serving as research participants, the procedures required by the research design, the method of collecting data, the type of data collected, or the nature of the research report. As a matter of fact, certain types of ethical difficulties occur repeatedly in social relations research. While scientists have an obligation to protect the participants in their research, they also have an obligation to contribute to knowledge. The need for knowledge relevant to the promotion of human welfare and the solution of social problems is particularly acute. Scientists who are trained to provide such knowledge violate the trust placed in them by society, if they do not take part in efforts to satisfy this need. Thus, when they consider abandoning a study (or using methods they think are not the best) they experience a value conflict. They must choose between their obligations to protect the welfare of their research subjects.

Sometimes, on the other hand, the balancing of costs and benefits of the research investigation will result in a discussion to carry it out. In this event, the investigator incurs obligations to the research participant following completion of the research. These obligations, for example, to clarify the nature of the research including the reasons for the research, to remove any harmful after effects of questionable used research, and to guarantee the subject's anonymity and the confidentiality of the data.

In any research investigation the initial obligation of the researcher is to weigh carefully the potential contributions of the proposed research against the costs of participants exposed to the questionable practices. If the researchers judge the theoretical practical benefits too limited to justify the costs, they should not conduct the research. If they judge the converse to be true, they should proceed, a decision not to act when the action is warranted is as morally reprehensible as a decision to act when action is not warranted.

Weighing the potential benefits of the research against its anticipated costs is necessarily subjective. Though it is possible to enumerate many of the points to be considered, we believe that the balancing process itself must remain a matter for the individual investigator. Some argue that, in reality, an investigator has no way to measure the value of a project against its costs to others who have not freely and knowingly consented to suffer those costs. However likely this may be, there seems no alternative to making the effort.

Among the potential benefits of a given research project are the following:

1. Advances in scientific theory that contributes to a general understanding of human behaviour. An example might be

a better understanding of the power of social influence to induce compliance and obedience.

2. Advances in knowledge of practical value to society. An example might be research on methods to increase the effectiveness of governmental leaders.
3. Gains for the research participant, such as increased self-understanding, satisfaction in making a contribution to science or to the solution of social problems, needed money or special privileges, knowledge of social sciences, biological sciences or of research methods, and so on.

The possible costs to the participant of various questionable practices in research include affronts to dignity, anxiety, shame, embarrassment, self-doubts, loss of trust in social relations, loss of autonomy and self-determination, and lowered self-esteem. In attempting to assess both the actuality and the seriousness of such costs, social scientists have turned to the research participants themselves. They have sought information in several ways. Some investigators, for example, have described studies involving questionable practices and asked respondents to judge the ethical quality of various aspects of the studies, including deception. Others have asked that questionable practices be rated on such dimensions as psychological discomfort or invasion of privacy.

The fact that scientist studying human behaviour needs people to take part in their research occasionally causes questionable practices to happen. Under some circumstances, they meet this need by involving subjects in research without their knowledge or consent. However, the potential research participant knows that research will take place.

Ideally consent should be obtained only after a potential subject has been given adequate information about the research in question. What we shall examine in this section is the point that consent to participate may be free or it may be wholly or partially coerced. The latter happens in several ways. For example, an investigator may be in a position to require individuals to participate. Sometimes, an employer or an institution may require participation of persons over whom they have authority. At other times, an investigator will offer such strong incentives that the potential participant is unable to resist, such as the case when Rs. 50 is offered to a poor person. In all such cases, the ideal of complete freedom of choice is abridged.

In extreme cases, as when persons are ordered by their employer or commanding officer to report for research, coercion is clear. In less extreme cases, however, it may be difficult to distinguish between coercion and legitimate persuasion or between coercion fair exchange of rewards and services.

When the freedom of individuals is restricted at their place of work or residence, such restrictions are likely to carry over into research done in these settings. Thus, employees, patients, prisoners, or soldiers may be required to participate in research projects. If a branch of a military service needs to find the sources of a morale problem, soldiers will be expected to take part in research without objecting. Or if an industry wishes to experiment with methods that may increase productivity, workers will be expected to participate. Similar expectations may hold for patients in mental hospitals with respect to research on therapeutic methods or prisoners with respect to procedures for rehabilitation.

It may be the case, however, that the potential participants are not in sympathy with the research objectives and would not take part if allowed to decide for them. The worker in the factory may see productivity research as a step toward greater exploitation, and the prisoner may feel that society, not he or she, needs changing. Under such circumstances, investigator faces a conflict between their desire, and often their obligation, to conduct potentiality significant research and the questionable practice of engaging people in research who have been completely or partially coerced to participate.

Three variations of this conflict may be distinguished; the ethical issues they posed are somewhat different. In an institution, first arises in a research project in which some features of the programme or the organization in question is being studied with a view to increasing its defectiveness. The second occurs in research that is meaningful only if carried out with the cooperation of a particular type of a person residing in an institution, for example; study of any type of mental illness. The third is encountered in research that utilizes participant from institutions or organizational settings. But has no relationships to the programme or to the people in the settings, for example, when prisoners are research participants in a study of group problem solving.

Unlike others who are involved in studies without their knowledge or consent, some individuals may willingly participate in a research project but not be told true intent. Usually, their participation is explained to these subjects in terms that although true, tell only part of the story. Misleading explanations of this kind have acquired the label, "cover story" they cover up the experiment's true nature. Their function is to satisfy and not misled as to the nature of the experiences they will have or the discomforts to be encountered.

When subjects consent to take part in research without being told its true characteristics, they are not giving what is commonly called their informed consent. This term had its origins in relation to medical treatment and research and designates patients' rights to consider a type of treatment or research participation with full knowledge of the risks to their personal safety as applied to social science research, the term has acquired connotations extending considerably beyond this original use.

Withholding information about research in which a person consents to participate is as questionable practice for reasons previously noted the right of free choice has been curtailed and, as a result, human dignity has been diminished. Social scientists are obliged to avoid such acts if at all possible. If they cannot, they must give careful consideration to the ethical costs of carrying out the research and the values to be served in so doing.

Most social scientists consider the version of informed consent to be both unnecessary and impractical. They feel that some aspects of a research plan are of little interest or concern to participants and those other more technical aspects are beyond their comprehension. Moreover, developments occur in the course of some research that could not be anticipated and, hence, could not be described to participants in advance. As a result, these social scientists favor a statement of principle that omits these undesirable features. The wording of the ethics code of one of the social science disciplines reflects this:

> Ethical practice requires the investigator to inform the participants of all features of the research that reasonably might be expected to influence willingness to participate, and to explain all other aspects of the research about which the participant inquires (APA, 1973).

Experience of researchers indicates that if they operate according to this second version of informed consent, they will find that most research participants are concerned about what will happen to them in the research, how long the research will take, and any inconveniences or risks that are involved. In contrast, most participants are unconcerned about the nature of the research question being asked and are as likely to be willing to answer one kind of question as another. (However, participants do judge research involving pain, stress, or undesirable behaviour as more ethical if they believe the research topic to be an important one).

A special questionarises over how the research results will be used. For example, some potential subjects would not willingly participate in research intended to increase war-making efficiency. Members of religious groups or ethnic groups would not wish to take part in the research if the results were expected to reflect discredit on their group. A researcher finds it difficult to respond to such concerns for two reasons. First, it is not always possible to predict the applied value of the research. Second, once the research results become public, the researcher has no way to control the use to which others put the findings.

It has been observed that the participants have been misled by withholding information from them, either about the fact that research was in progress or about the nature of it.

The distinction between deceiving others passively by telling only part of the truth versus actively by telling an untruth has little, if any moral standing, in our opinion. Nevertheless, social scientists take the latter more seriously because it brings an additional element into the picture, namely, a violation of participants' assumptions that they can trust what the researcher says. The ideal in the relationship between scientist and research participants is that of openness and honesty. Deliberate lying in the interest of manipulating the participant's perceptions and actions goes directly against this ideal. Yet often the choice appears to be between carrying out such deception and abandoning the research.

Even though the conduct of a research project has generated ethical questions in its treatment of research participants, the investigators incur certain obligation that must be fulfilled following its completion. Among these are the following: they must follow thoroughly on any commitments made to the participants when soliciting their cooperation, they must give them such additional information about the research and its results as they desire, and they must assure subject's anonymity and keep in confident subject's responses.

In addition, when the research has involved one or more of the ethical questions, the investigator incurs other obligations. For example, if the methodology requirements of the study have necessitated concealment or deception, the researcher must clarify to the research participant the reasons for this and restore a relationship of mutual trust and respect. If the research procedure has involved discomfort or stress or has diminished the participant's dignity or self-esteem, the investigator must do everything possible to alleviate such consequences.

In clarifying the true nature of the research that has involved concealment or deception, the investigator should strive to achieve the following:

1. Convey to the participants the investigator's sense of the potential value of the research.
2. Give the participants an appreciation of the contributions they have made to the research.
3. Provide the participants with an educational experience that includes an understanding of behavioural science research as used in the study in which they have taken part.
4. Develop in the participants an understanding of the necessity (as the investigator sees it) or employing questionable practices to obtain meaningful answers to the research question asked in the study.
5. Immunize the participants against the tendency for negative impressions of self that are developed in experiments to preservance even after attempts have been made to correct them.
6. Convince the participants of the investigator's regrets over the need to employ questionable practices and concern over the participants' feelings about having been subjected to these practices.
7. Give the research participants a perspective on their experiences that minimizes any feeling that they might have been manipulated, made fools of, shown to be gullible, or revealed character weaknesses.

The obligation to protect research participants' anonymity and keep research data in confidence is an all-inclusive one and should be fulfilled unless specific arrangements to the contrary are made by the participants themselves. Moreover, the more initiate and sensitive the responses and the less open the procedures by which they were gathered, the greater is the transgression in releasing them to others. When measures are obtained covertly and deal with private matters, the investigator incurs an especially heavy responsibility to keep them in confidence.

In deciding whether or not to promote the utilization of their research results, social scientists confront one or more of three ethical issues. One of these is whether an investigator has the responsibility for promoting such utilization; this is the counterpart to the issue of his or her responsibility for preventing the misuse of results. A second has to do with the timing of the application of research findings – in particular, whether the application may be premature. The third has to do with rectifying what many regard as an undemocratic imbalance in the utilization of research knowledge – an imbalance characterized by the greater availability of social science to those with educational and financial resources than those without.

Concluding Remarks

The proposition–that the research scientist is responsible for encouraging the application of this research results–draws support from two directions. The first is from the public. Support of social science of society is based not so much on an interest in knowledge for the sake of knowledge as it is in an interest in its practical utilization. The social scientist is looking primarily for his or her help in alleviating and preventing social problems and social conflict. The second direction is from the social scientist himself or herself. Many people enter the social sciences, in part because of their concern for human welfare. It is natural for them to ask whether their work contributes to its development. However, there is widespread opposition to the idea that the scientist has any special responsibility for research utilization. According to this view, the scientist's function is the production of knowledge. This knowledge is available to all, and it is the responsibility of practical people in society to apply it.

Among investigators who feel responsible for encouraging utilization of their research there will be differences of opinion on a second issue, that is, of timing. Some will feel that the possibility of utilization should be examined in connection with every study. Others will disagree, feeling that such attempts at application are premature. They argue that a theory based on many studies is the only sound basis for applying science. According to this view, attempts to base application of the results of single studies will mislead people who do not have scientific training and is, hence, an ethically questionable practice. To some extent, this difference of opinion may be minimized by considering the nature of the research. Immediate application will be justified when, for example, the researcher is studying a complex programmatic activity in a natural setting. One reason for this is that the similarity of the programme studied and the setting in which it was studied to other programmes is great enough to make generalizations appropriate. By comparison, laboratory studies aimed at developing an aspect of a theory will suggest little by way of immediate application. The results of such studies, in combination with other research, may later provide the social scientist with a basis for developing innovative programmes or new social institutions. However, not until such programmes or institutions are evaluated will it be timely to foster application under field conditions.

The third ethical issues have to do with the potential for differential utilization of research findings by different components of society. Large industries and government agencies have the resources to be alert to scientific developments and utilize them. Schools and public service agencies, owing to financial restrictions, have this capacity to a significantly lesser degree. Community groups and organization with low levels of economic and educational resources are the least well equipped to make use of potentially applicable research knowledge. Social scientists have recognized this and many have attempted to correct it. As yet, however, their efforts have met with only slight success.

Finally, I would suggest that the anthropologists in India should think the implications and future perspective of ethical issues so that there should be no complications in research and no political games be allowed to play every individual is benefited by any research which makes him/her "Happy and Smiling".

Acknowledgements

I am thankful to Ms. Vijeta Choudhary and Ms. Heemanshu Aurora, NN Fellow of Delhi University for going through the manuscript and editing the paper in the present shape.

References

APA (1973). *Ethical Principles in the Conduct of Research with Human Participants*, Washington DC: American Psychological Association.

Beals, R.L. (1967). Background Information on Problems of Anthropological Research and Ethics, *American Anthropological Association Fellow Newsletter* 8 (1): 1-13.

Indian Council of Medical Research (1997). *Consultative Document on Ethical Guidelines on Biomedical Research Involving Human Subjects* (Draft), New Delhi; ICMR.

Samantaray, S.K. and Gopal Sahu (2008). Ethical Issues and Challenges in Social Science Research in India. *Proceedings of International Conference on Survey Methods in Multinational, Multiregional, and Multicultural Contexts (3MC)*, Berlin, Germany; June 25-28, 2008.

CHAPTER 2

Ethics in Social Research

Issues in Perspective

RAJATSUBHRA MUKHOPADHYAY

In social science, ethical questions are intrinsic, ubiquitous and unavoidable. Anthropological and Sociological research normally takes place in a social context where the people (the informants) studied by the field workers are referred to as the objects of research or the subjects of experiment. While doing social surveys, the researchers often face variety of ethical problems in the field. Those are particularly on the question of what would be proper or improper, appropriate or inappropriate, or right or wrong on the part of his/her approach and behaviour while conducting field study. The scholars engaged in field research have gradually realized that every society is a moral community constituted of individuals who are equally moral beings, though they may culturally differ from their own. And why it is so essential to understand the ethical issues involved in empirical research and the moral implications of the field enquiry? The present chapter intends to offer some insights into the matter taking into consideration the issues in perspective.

I

There are a number of puzzles about the term 'ethics'. Let us look into some of the connotations of it. Terminologically, 'ethics' implies a culture of the rules of conduct which intimates us about the proper course of action on the part of a man. It is a branch of Philosophy that talks about ethical aspects of morality. Therefore, in the first instance, 'ethics' can be used simply as a synonym for 'morality'. It addresses the issues pertaining to morality particularly with reference to the question of 'values' attached to the concepts like good and evil, right and wrong etc. Secondly, 'ethics' is used to refer to 'codes of conduct' which consists partly of ordinary moral rules, partly of rules of etiquette, and partly of rules of professional conduct (Downie 1971:1). So the term 'professional ethics' refers to the moral responsibility of a professional towards the society while providing service to the public. Or, to put it in another way, 'professional ethics' are standards of codes of conduct for people in a particular profession and professionally what they should and should not do in their work in which they are engaged.

The codes of professional ethics lay down the standards of integrity, professionalism and confidentiality of all the members engaged in a specific job. If we turn now to compare the aim of Sociology and kindred social sciences (including Anthropology) with that of the social ethics, we find that the sociological enquiries aim at providing knowledge about how people behave or act in social contexts, and about how social institutions operate in given societies at given times. And on consideration of the latter (ethics) while conducting sociological enquiries on social institutions and behaviour what should be the ethically appropriate behaviour? There are, however, disagreements among the sociologists on the question of ethically appropriate or inappropriate behaviour (Allen 1997).

While studying any form of human behaviour, ethical questions are unavoidable. Ideally, research codes of ethics address individual rights to dignity, privacy and confidentiality; and avoidance of harm. Here one may note that close observation of others' behaviour, thoughts, and feelings, making public that which is typically private can cause hurt, pain and harm to them. For instance, as observed by Babbie; given the highly personal nature of sexuality and society's tremendous concern with social control of sexuality, the right to privacy is an important ethical concern for research in this area. Individuals may risk losing jobs, having family difficulties, or being ostracized by press if certain facts of their sexual lives are revealed (2004: 70). Therefore, it is essential that the researchers should understand the ethically sensitive issues and the implications of their enquiry, and also to act accordingly. They further need to respect human rights of the participants of research.

Persons engaged in social research required to be made aware of the general agreements shared by scholars about what is proper and what is improper in the conduct of social enquiry. The researchers, therefore, must take into account many ethical points in designing and executing their research. The method of giving fictitious names to the informants or even to a study village is an age-old technique in ensuring confidentiality to the information provided by an informant to the researcher. One may wonder to know that the original name of the much acclaimed village studied by M.N. Srinivas in Mysore was Kodagahalli and not Rampura. Possibly Srinivas assigned this fictitious name to his study village on ethical ground.

II

The issue of ethics in social sciences, unlike medical sciences, has been given less prominence in India. Perhaps no social science in India has a code of professional ethics or for that matter any comprehensive guideline for the same. A researcher is rarely informed or made educated about his expected code of conduct while doing fieldwork. While admitting the fact that all field workers face variety of ethical problems in the field of sociology, A.M. Shah expressed his disappointment and asked: "Who will enforce the code, and how"? (2006: 3). Although social science institutions in India have many directives for improving the quality of research but they hardly offer any ethical guidelines for field based research. It is however important to note that most professional associations of social sciences (including sociology and anthropology) in developed countries have already formulated and refined their ethical guidelines of research.

Noted anthropologist M.N. Srinivas and his associates observed that intensive fieldwork also bristles with moral problems. It is difficult to avoid them and these moral problems are insoluble. A section of others, however, believe that there is a way out (1979: 10). Thus, the questions pertaining to ethical aspects of social research kept on oscillating and remain unanswered or unsettled. While arguing on ethical questions in social sciences, Barnes observed that in most instances of social research ethical comprises are unavoidable (1996: 180). The available codes of guidelines generally led to the impression that a perfect solution exists to every ethical problem. And to ensure that the most common and humble prescription is—the fieldworker must be honest, must respect the interests of all respondents, and like. Barnes however felt that this impression is misleading, as in most instances of empirical inquiry no perfect solution is available (*Ibid:* 186).

Social scientists do not always agree on the point of ethically appropriate or inappropriate behaviour. Practicing professional ethics in Sociological and Anthropological research is therefore challenging. There is need to recognize that the cultural background, economic, social and political factors often influence the ethical standard of any professional community and even of a researcher.

From the point of view of Sociology and Anthropology and the study of other culture, the primary ethical consideration demands respect from the investigator towards the people of alien culture; while any attempt to despise them implies disrespect. So in the conception of Srinivas—"the one who considers the values and customs of his own culture right and proper in comparison to those of another culture is guilty of ethical arrogance" (Srinivas *et al.* 1979: 12). But as it happens, when an anthropologist/sociologist (being urban, educated and forward looking) studies a tribal community with a code of moral and ethical values differing dramatically from his own, he started suffering from some kind of ethical dilemmas. Similarly, one also could not refuse to take a moral stand with regard to the problems of say poverty, deprivation or exploitation. All these issues and examples constitute a part of that contradiction where the relation between the local value system and the system of values held by the fieldworker who possesses a rational, educated, forward looking progressive mind do not corroborate. Hence, the mere replacement of 'ethical arrogance' by say an 'ethical submissiveness' of a researcher can hardly resolve the ethical dilemma involved in the process.

Ethics of social research asks a field investigator to subordinate many of his norms and judgments to those of the community who are under his study. For instance, a researcher may personally favour small family norm but in response to the problem of overpopulation he wants to conduct a survey on fertility to determine why some people go for more children and others don't? In this situation what personal involvement problems a researcher would face and how could he/ she avoid them? What ethical stand should the researcher take into account in advancing and designing the fertility survey? Or for instance, should a researcher openly make known his disapproval of certain native practices like infanticides, witch-hunting, child marriage, polygyny etc. which offend and horrify him, or should he seek refuse behind moral relativism? (*Ibid*: 10). In such cases, the ethics of the social enquiry and the application of the expertise of social science to current social problem need to be dealt with.

III

There has been a continuing debate between the view of making of social sciences 'value free' and 'objective'. But the general sentiment is that social scientists could not remain value free simply because they deal with societal issues and because there is an explicit connection between research and social action or political view-point. Besides abstract disagreement as to whether social science can or should be value free, Babbie remarked that although most researchers agree that political orientation should not unduly influence researcher, in practice it can be quite difficult to separate politics and ideology from the conduct of research (2004: 81). However, in such situations, the ethics of the social enquiry altogether acquires a different significance and is predicted against the general sentiment that a researcher's personal political orientation should not interfere with or unduly influence his/her scientific enquiry. Both ethics and politics hinge on ideological point of view. Although, ethical and political issues are often closely intertwined but from all practical considerations they are distinguishable. While the ethics of social research deals mostly with the methods employed, the political issues tend to centre on the substance and use of research. Moreover, even when some ethical norms have political aspects but there are no formal codes of accepted political behaviour. No one has developed a set of political norms that all social researchers accept (Babbie, *Ibid:* 75-76).

On the question of neutrality of research in social sciences, we may note that it can never be totally objective, because researchers are basically human beings and therefore necessarily subjective. Max Weber's 'value free sociology' (1946) urged that sociology, like other sciences, needed to be unencumbered if it was to make a special contribution to society. In the contrary, Marxist and neo-Marxist scholars have argued that social science and social action cannot and should not be separated. According to their opinion, merely studying society and its ills without a commitment to making society more humane has been called irresponsible.

Though the ethical and political dimensions of social research are in principle distinct, they do intersect. The intrusion of political and related ideologies is not unique to social research. The natural sciences have also experienced similar situations. The image of 'science' as intrinsically neutral, beneficial, and value-free was eroded around World War-II with revelations of the Nuremberg trials recounting the Nazis' medical experiment on concentration camps inmates. With the disclosure of instances of unethical investigations in medical research and social science since 1960s, 'ethics' emerged as a central issue in research (Bresler 1995) particularly with reference to 'moral' questions.

IV

There is another side of the problem. Extreme career considerations often influence the ethical standard of any professional community. The problems are more acute in the case of social sciences referred to as 'soft' science than that of the natural or 'hard' science. Here the hard fact is that a sociologist or anthropologist does fieldwork basically to advance his career and not to benefit those whom he studies. So we do not get surprised when the respondents hesitate to take him in confidence and started asking—"What's in this for me? Why should I answer your questions?" Incidences are not rare when the so called primitive and non-literate respondents refuse to reveal their secrets to a probing field investigator, who is not an intimate member of the community, out of an apprehension that he would pass on the secrets to the greater society through his reports etc.

Sheer career considerations often provoked some persons in profession to undertake research without any proper motivation to sincerely work on it. They prefer to follow fast data collection techniques and 'touch and go' type of field survey for quicker preparation of theses, reports, papers etc., required for academic promotion or for other benefits available out of Career Advancement Schemes. Such researchers, according to Srinivas, did not enjoy their fieldwork but develop a dislike (least empathy) for the people they were studying (2004: 547-48).

In addition to institutional limitations, lack of time and empathy, non-involvement, formal and more mechanical conversation relationship, concern for status and cultural differences between the researcher and the informant, all greatly contributed to the frequent violation of ethical norms in the field. That also led to dilution of the time tested intensive fieldwork tradition in India (Mukhopadhyay 2000). Some foresighted social scientists began to take account of the fact that all these are very much part of the ethical problem and such type of social enquiry often disturbs the phenomenon that is being investigated.

Different categories of persons, in different capacities, do participate in research. Their nature of commitment to research work differs substantially. This often poses a serious problem to the ethical question in social research. Many of them, particularly those who are aspiring for Ph.D. degree for personal promotion through CAS or FIP schemes introduced by UGC are neither bothered about the ethical aspects of empirical research, nor about their professional integrity. They are always in a great hurry and suffer from lack of time. Their quick visit to field sometimes lasts only a few days, and seldom more than a few weeks. They cannot stand the strain of isolation, especially in what are often uncomfortably and unhealthy conditions. Such field investigators rarely become emotionally involved with the people they are studying, and hardly think about how their approach/conduct could affect them, or more so what is to be ethically proper while in the field.

Now a days, social science research in India becomes more sponsor's dependent. Other than UGC and ICSSR, a large number of government, semi-government and private agencies/ organizations are, in diverse capacities, sponsoring social surveys to meet up their non-academic objectives and business needs. Serious ethical problems arise when these bodies try to pressurize an institute or an individual scholar to take up a certain ideological line or to monitor results of research according to their wishes. These organizations might also try to influence research by favouring institution/individuals by providing grants and fellowships (Shah 2006: 3). All these tactics certainly pose a serious threat to the ethics of social research and call for our immediate attention.

V

At the outset, I must say that any discussion on ethics in social research is inconclusive. Professional codes and guidelines often led to the impression that a perfect solution is there to counter every ethical problem. But that is not the reality. The ethical problems in social research are normally addressed from the perspectives of field tactics rather than pure 'ethics', as the fieldworkers are often encountered with moral problems.

Basically 'ethics' refers to codes of conduct which consist partly of rules of etiquette, and partly of professional conduct. Being a part of 'moral philosophy', codes of ethics in social research denote individual right to dignity, privacy, confidentiality, and avoidance of harms. The argument is—close study of others' activities and behaviour (which are absolutely private), for the sake of research and later making them known to others through publications can cause hurt, pain and harm to them. It is therefore expected that the researchers should try to understand the ethical issues involved in the fieldwork and the moral implications of their enquiry.

The ethical issues in social research have given less prominence in India. Perhaps no social science in India has a code of professional ethics. Although social science institutions in India have many guidelines for improving the quality of research but possibly there is nothing on professional ethics. Surprisingly, a very few books or articles examine what and how to teach about ethics to the students engaged in social research? The effort to formulate ethical guidelines for research in social sciences and health in India began only in 1998 under the title of *Ethical Guidelines for Social Science Research in Health* by a team of nine members headed by Prof. Ghanshyam Shah, a distinguished Political Scientist.

Unfortunately, the ethical issues in social sciences in India hardly occupy any serious place in the academic discourses. It is rather left to the individual researcher to regulate on his own and evolve his own codes of conduct. In the absence of any comprehensive guidelines, ethical questions are often ignored in our social science research. That further led to frequent violation of basic ethical norms and dilution of field research. Sheer careerist considerations often provoked a section of aspirant professionals to opt for 'fast research' and also in writing orderly 'rapid-appraisals' against sponsor projects ignoring all ethical norms in conducting field surveys. A category of social scientists have now urged upon to immediately take up ethical issues involved in social research with all seriousness in order to respect and protect human rights and dignity of the participants of research and at the same time in ensuring professional integrity.

References

Allen, Charlotte. (1997). Spies Like Us: When Sociologists Deceive Their Subjects. *Lingua Franca* 7 (9): 31-39.

Babbie, Earl (2004). *The Practice of Social Research* (10th Ed.). Chennai: Thomson Wadsworth (India Edition).

Barnes, John A. (1996). Unavoidable Compromises in Social Research. *In*: A.M. Shah, B.S. Baviskar and E.A. Ramaswamy (Eds.), *Social Structure and Change* (Vol. I). New Delhi: Sage Publications, pp. 178-196.

Bresler, Liora (1995). Ethical Issues in Qualitative Research Methodology. *Bulletin of the Council for Research in Music Education*, 126 (Fall), pp. 29-41.

Downie, R.S. (1971). *Roles and Values: An Introduction to Social Ethics*. London: Methuen & Co. Ltd.

Mukhopadhyay, Rajatsubhra (2007). Contextualizing Fieldwork in Indian Anthropology. *In*: Sanjoy K. Roy and Ajit K. Danda (Eds.), *Methodological Questions in Social Anthropology*. Jhargram: Indian National Confederation and Academy of Anthropologists (INCCA), pp. 110-124.

Shah, A.M. (2006). Ethics in Sociological and Social Anthropological Research: A Brief Note. *eSocialSciences Conference Paper: Ethics in Social Sciences July 2006.*

Srinivas, M.N. (2004). "The Observer and the Observed in the Study of Cultures and Participant Observation." *In:* M.N. Srinivas (Ed.) *Collected Essays*. Delhi: Oxford University Press.

Srinivas, M.N., A.M. Shah and A.E. Ramaswamy (Eds.), (1979). *The Fieldworker and the Field: Problems and Challenges in Sociological Investigation*. Delhi: Oxford University Press.

Weber, Max (1946). Science as a Vocation. *In*: Hans Gerth and C. Wright Mills (Eds.), *From Max Weber: Essays in Sociology*. New York: Oxford University Press, pp. 129-56.

CHAPTER 3

Ethical Issues in Ethno-Archaeological Research

SOM PRASAD KHATIWADA

Introduction

Ethical issue is related with morality of researchers that helps to bring accuracy in research work and protection of human rights, which is usually advocated by research scholars. It is a code of conduct for researchers that are to be followed. It is not a rigid rule and barrier that is punishable by the law, while violating or breaking it. So, it depends upon the morality and attitude of a researcher. Research is systematic finding of new knowledge from the help of facts collected as the sources or evidences. The method of studying human behaviour in different disciplines is the same with slightly difference in its framework. Study of ethnicity is a branch of social research that is done within a certain framework. In this context, archaeology is a branch of anthropology in term of its subject matter, i.e. human being. One is related with the study of human nature, whereas other seeks the material remains of the past as evidences. Archaeological excavation is the means of finding artifacts or antiquities as the source of data from historical sites. Exploration helps to locate rich archaeological sites. Study area of this discipline is not so far from human culture and his behaviour. In the same way, anthropology is the science of studying human being, which is not so far with archaeology. Study of ethnicity from the help of archaeological materials is called Ethno-archaeology or anthropological archaeology.

While exploring the new knowledge in archaeology, anthropology and ethnography the ethical issues are usually forgotten by the researchers. Finding new knowledge from an ordinary material of the past is a great challenge for them. It is very risky to analyze antiquities in the sense that there is a great possibility of errors and its erection also is not so easy. In the same way, the researchers do not care on positive and negative aspects of human behaviour. The question of human rights does not arise in such a research. Instead, need of preservation and conservation of the artifacts excavated out from the earth is necessary for coming generation. Therefore, it is one of the most important issues of ethics for the researcher.

In the context of modern human right ethical issue is divided in global and local aspects. In global aspect protection of antiquities for further generation is expected. Proper exploration of archaeological potential sites and their excavation is expected without caring political boundaries. Every people have the same kind of right to know the historical importance of their territories. In the same way, selling of data and forgery of antiquities for personal benefit should be controlled. Role of NGOs for collecting imaginary data according to their need should also be controlled.

Introduction of Ethno-Archaeology

Ethnography is a science of studying different aspects of ethnic groups. There are thousands of ethnic groups settled from the long period in Indian sub-continent. Different ethnic groups seem different with separate physical features, their customs and cultures. Different ethnic groups inside Mongoloid, Caucasoid, Negroid and other racial groups reside in this region. Some ethnic groups have their living society, while the others have cut-off by the process of migration for food gathering activities. Ethnicity with living culture bears their traditional values and cut-off group do not have such situation.

Archaeology is the science of studying ancient man and his culture from the help of material remains. Hence, both ethnography and archaeology are related with the study of man and his behaviour. But they are differentiated in the way that one does not care for the time limit, whereas other is mainly related with the past. In the same way, ethnography studies both kind of societies having living culture and their history. But archaeology does not care for the study of present culture and society. Therefore, ethno-archaeology is a science that studies ancient ethnic groups from the help of material remains of their past. Archaeology provides evidences for ethnography for the study of mankind and the other calculates their culture with comparison. Therefore, ethno-archaeology is a combined discipline of studying ancient man and their culture. In short, archaeology is the means of finding facts and ethnography is for defining and explaining it.

Modern Indian culture has long root in prehistory (Fagan, 1994). Long cultural trails are developed in this subcontinent from prehistoric period. Material remains found from the time of Ramapithecian culture shows its deep-rooted existence in this sub-continent. Comparison of archaeological data is possible from the finding of living archaeology in this region. Therefore, different scholars of the world are interested to study ethno-archaeology in India and surrounding countries.

Ethno-archaeology is not limited with time and area of study. It starts from the origin of man and reaches up to the present man and his society. With physical development of man it covers human society and culture of the past. But it is not interested with present society and culture. Study of present man and his society is the continuation of ancient man and his culture. Therefore, archaeologists and anthropologists both work in the same field to identify ancient man and his culture.

Anthropologists study human beings as biological organism and as people with a distinctive and unique characteristic culture (Fagan, 1994). It is related with study of human evolution and his phenomena in the context of development. It is a broad aspect of studying humanity. Physical as well as social and cultural anthropology covers the large area of study. Archaeologists are also special types of anthropologists, whose interest of study does not go out from man and his behaviour (Fagan, 1994). Therefore, a great controversy between these two groups of discipline is not solved from a long time (Kroeber and Kluckhohn, 1952). But both of them seek the central point of controversy and try to reduce its conflict. In this context, Tylor had given a unique definition of culture to reduce it. He says, "culture is that complex whole which includes knowledge, belief, art, morals, law, custom and any other capabilities and habits acquired by man as a member of society" (Tylor, 1871). In fact, culture is all primary means of adapting to our environment (Fagan, 1994). Hence, physical anthropology does not concern more on human behaviour and culture. But it is related with man and the man is connected with the culture. Culture is the primary means of adapting to the environment. Culture is a buffer between us and the environment. For example, the polar bear has got thick hair to adopt the environment, because it does not have its culture to adopt with it. But an Inuit use igloo and thick animal leather or wool to adopt with environment. Such behaviour can help us to dominate the environment in the different parts of the world with distinct climate. But lack of such knowledge, animals can survive only in suitable environment. Human being has modified natural environment to make it suitable for its existence whereas the animals have modified themselves as the nature for their survival. Such conditions may be covered by both archaeologists and anthropologists.

Ethical Issues

Ethnology is close with the study of living culture which is related with living archaeology also. Ethnicity is the continuation of human society in certain area with their unique culture. Not only cultural aspect, the physical aspect of the ethnic groups also remains the same for a long span of time. Physical as well as the cultural anthropologists show their interest to study such groups. Archaeologists investigate their remains and compare them with the artifacts of living culture and society. Their findings can help them to trace the changing of their habit, artifact and old equipments. Therefore, finding of old artifacts is the starting point of archaeological studies and pointing out the cultural relation with such artifact turns to the study area of anthropology. Therefore, ethno-archaeological study cannot go beyond anthropology and archaeology. Ethical issue arises for both disciplines.

While talking about ethno-archaeology, we can see its direct impact to the modern society. For example, we can take Maya civilization, which was developed in physical as well as the spiritual background (Feder, 1990). Traditional concept of that civilization has affected some ethnic groups even today. Information of ending their calendar date from December 2012 has become a great fear among different groups. Means of communication are raising this issue as an important message. Archaeologists as well as the anthropologists should communicate the reality of such events up to the ethnic society, which is also ethical issue in ethno-archaeological studies.

Multidisciplinary research team should be managed for ethno-archaeological studies. They should communicate each other about finding materials and research findings (Isaac and Isaac, 1989). It helps to understand the all aspect of human behaviour from the material remains of man's past. Recording experts, photographers and other experts can play vital role in ethno-archaeological studies

(Dorrell, 1989). Therefore, the ethical issue of ethno-archaeological study is related to group work.

When considering the ethical issues in ethno-archaeological studies, the following points should be mentioned:

(i) Proper exploration and excavation of historical and prehistoric sites should be done.

(ii) It should be done in global context not limiting to the developed countries.

(iii) Scholars from both developed and developing countries should work with together for the study of man and their culture in a joint team.

(iv) The system of purchasing and selling data on ethno-archaeology should be avoided.

(v) Ethical issues should be maintained by the scholars, respondents and other related bodies while doing archaeological, anthropological and ethno-archaeological research.

(vi) The system of doing ethnic studies in the frame provided by the donor agencies should be discouraged. This system affects to the method of study, which is normally used for the academic research. But the donor agencies develop different methodological framework to fulfill their target and the limited fund is provided to the researchers. It helps to gather the information in their favour. The system of manipulating data begins from their activities. Therefore, research activities should not be guided by NGO framework. Instead they should be guided by research norms, values and methodology.

(vii) It is better to save the archaeological sites as virgin land than the excavation activities done without proper planning, because excavation results the damage of antiquities and the archaeological sites.

(viii) Proper testing, preserving and collecting of antiquities should be done after excavation.

(ix) Forgery in prehistoric tools and their finding should be totally controlled by the rule of different countries.

(x) Proper rules and regulations should be made and implemented by the countries to preserve antiquities and sites of archaeological values.

(xi) Tendency of grave hunter of some developing countries should be discouraged.

(xii) Study of anthropology should be prioritized by different countries as a subject with international value.

Ethno-archaeology is related with the finding of antiquities and the study of human behaviour of the past. Therefore, the source of the study is material remain of man's past. They are found from different strata of the earth, which are collected under the surface of the earth formatted regularly in the surface. When an archaeologist excavates the archaeological sites, the serial of strata destroyed and order of finding the material remains disorders. Therefore, doing excavation without proper planning is not expected by archaeologists. It depends upon the ethics of an excavator. The excavated sites should be protected in the proper way to keep it in original form. Conservation and preservation of the findings is another duty of an excavator. Generally, collected archeological antiquities are placed in the museums. Special consideration on these artifacts should be done to carry them up to the museum. Field laboratory is another item that should be managed before excavation. The artifacts should be washed out clearly and tested in the lab. Different kinds of chemicals and equipments are used to test these artifacts.

Some of the archaeological sites are excavated without proper planning and the antiquities are destroyed in some countries. Ethics of excavation is not followed properly in such spots which leads to great loss of knowledge on ethno-archaeology. Forgery of artifacts and misunderstanding of archeological sites is another issue that should be discouraged by the government. Attempt of establishing a native land as an important historical site can become a hobby for some people. Forgery in data is also done by such people. Proper law of a country can discourage such activities. Legends and history of such places should be studied properly before dating the artifacts from the sites.

Most of important archaeological sites are excavated properly in developed countries. But such sites of underdeveloped countries are not excavated properly even today. That is the main cause of lacking knowledge on ethno-archaeology. Despite of having important historical and prehistoric sites in developing countries, the governments of these countries are not succeeded for the exploration and excavation of these sites. The ethics of archaeologists remains more important in such a country. They should excavate them with the limited resource or protect the sites properly for further excavation.

The local issues on ethics related on ethno-archaeological study is that most of the prehistoric sites of developing countries are still unknown. Limited studies conducted by foreign scholars on prehistory in such countries are not sufficient. Most of such studies are done for their own benefit. Most of the artifacts are stolen and others are lost in the process of such studies in developing countries. Prehistoric data and antiquities of archaeological importance are bought and sold for their personal benefit. For example, most of the ancient art objects of developing countries are sold to the museums of developed countries; which is great loss not only for developing countries, but for the human being of the whole world. It becomes our ethics to control such activities.

Concluding Remarks

Archaeology as a branch of anthropology provides data for the study of ancient man. They are collected from different strata of land which are formatted from the long geological process. Exploration and excavation are main two methods to find such data. Ethical issues remain the most important part for the study of prehistoric and ancient man. Due to the limited availability of evidences for the study of that period, there is a great risk of loosing and misusing them. Loss of an archaeological site is a great loss of the history of mankind. In the same way, manipulation of data may misinform the whole history and civilization. Therefore, the locals, researchers, governments and intellectuals are expected to follow the ethics of preserving and preventing archaeological sites for the study of man for further generation.

Different activities may destroy the archaeological evidences. Urbanization, digging pit and ponds in the land, making roads, railways, airports and other activities may cover out the archaeological antiquities from the land. Inside the land, they remain safe, but they start to decay after covering out them in the surface of the land. Therefore, the researchers, locals and other concerned persons should protect these as the properties of our ancestors. If we preserve, it will become the property for future generation. Such process depends upon our ethics.

References

Dorrell, P. (1989). *Photography in Archaeology and Conservation*, Cambridge: Cambridge University Press.

Fagan, B.M. (1994). *In the Beginning: An Introduction to Archaeology*, New York: Harper Collins.

Feder, K.L. (1990). *Frauds, Myths and Mysteries: Science and Pseudoscience in Archaeology*, Mountain View, Calif: Mayfield Pub. Co.

Isaac, G.L. and B. Isaac (1989). *The Archaeology of Human Origins*, Cambridge: Cambridge University Press.

Kroeber, A.L. and C. Kluckhohn (1952). *Culture: A Critical Review of Concepts and Definitions*, Cambridge, MA: Harvard University Press.

Tylor, E.B. (1871). *Primitive Culture*, London: John Murray.

Chapter 4

Ethics and Anthropological Fieldwork

Problems and Consequences

Vijay Prakash Sharma

Introduction

Anthropology is basically field based science and as a part of research brings the researcher closest to the subject of research. It is a dynamic process where there is an exchange between the researcher, participants, stakeholders, gatekeepers, the community and the larger socio-political context in which the research problem is located. Ethical dilemmas that surface during fieldwork often pose a unique challenge to the researcher. Case studies offer another way to heighten sensitivity and improve anthropological practice. An ethical dilemma may be difficult to recognize when encountered; "practical" decisions frequently turn out to have ethical ramifications. Reading and thinking about situations faced by other anthropologists can help us to recognize our own ethical dilemmas and to make sensitive and informed decisions. To improve the ethical adequacy of anthropological practice, we must consider not only exceptional cases but everyday decisions, and reflect not only upon the conduct of others but also upon our own actions.

This chapter is based on field experiences during an action-research study conducted with Pahari Korwa tribe of Madhya

Pradesh, India. It discusses the role conflict that researchers face during fieldwork in a situation of humanitarian crisis. It raises issues pertaining to the need to extend the ethical decision-making paradigm to address ethical dilemmas arising during the course of fieldwork. The study was an action-research project; apart from documenting and studying the implications of resettlement on the community's habitat, work, and social life, it was also aimed at supporting the community's efforts to address its own concerns and needs post resettlement. The fieldwork raised certain key concerns. First, researchers were faced with a conflict of roles during data collection—the role of a researcher versus that of an intervener. Second, researchers faced unanticipated ethical dilemmas during the course of fieldwork. Sufficient preparation prior to fieldwork helps anticipate social, psychological and economic risks and, therefore, the possibility of resolving ethical dilemmas with the help of the ethics framework.

Process of Intervention: The Applied and Action Anthropology (AAA) Approach

The Applied and Action Anthropology approach is the intervention process where an action anthropologist can combine both action and research.

According to Vidyarthi (1978), "the scope of research in the field of applied research in India is very wide especially when the whole traditional society is in the process of large scale transformation. In proportion to the magnitude of the task; the output to the applied social anthropologists and sociologists has not been adequate. Though, role of the social anthropologists and other behavioural scientists in the various fields of national reconstruction is acknowledged, their impact and contributions have not been as desired. There are many reasons for such a situation of applied social sciences in this country. The role of social anthropologists has not been well defined in the bureaucratic machinery of the State and Central Governments. There is no unanimity even among the anthropologists themselves regarding their roles as analysts, advisers, and co-operators. It seems that the applied social scientists in India should gracefully accept the various roles suggested above if certain conditions are satisfied. Firstly, he should have appropriate status in organizational setup, and secondly, once a subject for investigation is agreed upon through consultation, he must be free to draw up design and the tools of investigations, and thirdly, he must be able to present his findings at the highest policy level."

Writing on categories of applied anthropologists in India Vidyarthi (1978:176-177) clarify five types such as:

I. Those that act as consultants on the staff of administration and usually function under the control of the administrators.
II. The second types are those who are consultants primarily to the administrators but are outsiders, i.e. they are not on the regular pay roll of the organization.
III. The researcher and administrator work together as co-administrators.
IV. A social anthropologist is at least temporarily in actual charge of the development programme of a community which he and his associates are studying.
V. The fifth category is represented by action anthropology of Sol Tax which can function only in an independent manner and in institutions where an action anthropologist can combine both action and research.

Applied and action anthropology approach a successful effort in the fifth category to bridge the gap between knowledge and practice that is the felt need of the hour to have a clear understanding of contemporary situation of the above mentioned primitive tribal groups in ecological setting of Jashpur District of

Chhattisgarh for better planning and implementation of need based development programmes by the district authorities.

It was proposed in 1997 that an Applied and Action Anthropology programme be commissioned urgently to study contemporary life and culture of these people with special emphasis on their ecology and problems and to implement some kind of development project to better their lives.

Author as a senior Anthropologist from G.G. University, Bilaspur, started Applied and Action Anthropology intervention programme among *Pahari Korwa* of Bagicha and Manora block in 1997 in collaboration with Tribal and Rural Development Institute of Jashpurnagar, Madhya Pradesh (now Chhattisgarh).

Regular interaction resulted into confidence building. A Socio-Economic survey was carried out to know their problems and with the help of local government many developmental programmes were implemented by the Institute.

Participatory Rural Appraisal (PRA) exercises were conducted; training programmes were organized to bring these hill dwellers in the mainstream of national life. A great tribal congregation of *Pahari Korwa* was organized at *Harrapat* in 2000 where the institute developed the idea of bringing them on plains as plain settlers.

Regular interaction resulted into confidence building particularly among vulnerable tribal group *Pahari Korwa* of Chhattisgarh. Counselling exercises were conducted; training programmes were organized to bring these hill dwellers in the main stream of national life by rehabilitating them on plains.

After long persuasion 13 families agreed to settle down on plains. The Institute convinced government to sanction PTG Housing scheme for them. Finally, thirteen families themselves volunteered to construct their own houses. A cherished dream of TRDI, under Applied and Action Anthropology Programme became reality in 2004.

Now, it was important to introduce livelihood development programme for these particularly vulnerable tribal group *Pahari*

Korwa of Chhattishgarh. For this, the institute implemented an UNDP supported Technology Management Programme (TMP). Under this programme, the institute has established block level Technology Resource Center (TRC) for Jashpur block in collaboration with Regional Research Laboratory, Bhopal. Technology, employment and tribal each one of these terms has baffled and divided both the academicians and the practitioners since long, especially during last few decades. Gurnar Myrdal, commenting on employment policy, emphasized in his epic study about Asia that, "If by a miracle, the cultivators in South Asia could be induced to work more diligently, production would rise dramatically."

Technology has been widely acknowledged as a critical parameter in the production system. Generally speaking in a broader sense of the term, it has been identified practically with each and every aspect involved in the process of development or change, in fact technology represents in a way the unending human struggle for a better existence in his/her environment.

If employment is to be generated in a tribal region, it should be and can be best done by promoting and strengthening the existing modes of production of the people with the inputs of modern science and technology in a manner that the advantages of the existing system as well as those created by men to exploit the resources are combined. The basic idea behind the project was to promote the traditional occupation and to introduce people's friendly new rural technology, upgrading of their skills, provision of raw materials and modern equipments, credit support and marketing facility for the development of livelihood of rural and tribal people. In specific terms, the project aimed at setting up a common facility centre for training, demonstration and popularization of small scale industrial packages for identified cluster of six villages in Manora block.

To strengthen the existing units under initial stage and to introduce new technologies that is tested in other tribal areas, two institutions UNDP and IFAD were approached through

Government of Madhya Pradesh and Government of Chhatisgarh, Tribal and Rural Development Institute adopted some villages under UNDP programme and introduced Mushroom production, Bee-keeping, Beehive box manufacturing, Production of Herbal pesticides, Production of fishing trap, Cultivation and storage of medicinal plants, Wooden handicraft, Beating drum *(Mandar)* production, Bamboo basket production, Broom making and marketing, Leaf mat, Leaf bowl and Leaf plate production etc. were introduced in the Cluster of 25 tribal dominated villages in Manora block of Jaspur district.

In the second step, International Fund for Agricultural Development (IFAD) sanctioned watershed projects covering 6 villages for three years duration, Micro watershed code 4G2B6G-1. Total geographical area of the Watershed was 1109.214 hectares out of which750.826 hectares were treatable area. There were 299 households inhabited by 1714 people (Male-884, Female-830).

The institute completed three years **Shaila Watershed Project** (2003-6) covering Six villages sanctioned by CGTDP, Government of Chhattisgarh, funded by International Fund for Agricultural Development (IFAD) and undertook following important activities:

1. 15 days training to 20 farmers on Fish Farming and Nylon net weaving.
2. Seven days training to 80 farmers on Bee-keeping.
3. Two months training to two persons on Bee-box making skill.
4. Fifty two farmers were trained on Vermi-compost and construction of permanent pit.
5. Four farmers were trained in PAIRRA Treatment.
6. Three Anganwadi centres, one each in Shaila, Chattauri and Chirotoli village were constructed.
7. One EGS building was constructed at village Kardana.

8. Two water ponds were constructed at village Chattauri and are used for fisheries.
9. Sixteen Indira Awas for Primitive Tribal Group (Pahari Korwa) were constructed in village Chattauri. This is first ever novel attempt to inhabit hill dwellers on plain. The sixteen Pahari Korwa families themselves contributed their labour in construction of their own houses. This is one of the most successful programmes of the Institute.
10. Construction of 207 meters RRC village approach road at village Shaila using local MLA fund.
11. Under Goat Farming activity 45 goats were distributed to 14 Shelf Help Groups for pursuing sustained livelihood.
12. Construction of 14 Goat sheds in PTG colony of Chattauri village.
13. Building for Vocational Training Centre was constructed at Village Chattauri.
14. Construction of one Stop-check-dam with canal at village Shaila.
15. Vegetable mini kits were distributed to 60 farmers.
16. 600 kgs Potato seeds were distributed among 34 members of BPL-SHGs.
17. 25 women were trained in Bamboo craft through three months training programme.
18. 40 women were provided training in Tailoring and Knitting works and they are earning livelihood through these skills.

Discussion

Results of the activities taken under AAA programme are clearly visible. In last Monsoon season, earthen and check-dams constructed by the Institute provided protective irrigation in moisture stress. In canal constructed area some farmers took up two crops this year against one earlier. Some farmers extended their area of Kharif crops. Tanks constructed by institute helped in fish farming and supplementary irrigation. Boulder and earthen checks proved to be of great help in checking soil erosion in the area. Construction of proper approach road in village Chattauri is of great help in transport and communication to villagers. The impact of Applied and Action Anthropology intervention may be summarized as follows:

1. Regular saving habits inculcated among members.
2. Several members increased their income adopting income generating activities promoted by the institute.
3. Easy access to financial services ensured.
4. Collective decision-making promoted by institute now institutionalized.
5. SHG members taking up community development works.
6. Women are running Fare Price Shops successfully in the area.

The demonstration effect of transparency and timely payment of wages in the programmes run by TRDI generated high faith and enthusiasm among the tribal community. Migration appears to have lowered down in comparison to previous years due to Creation of wage employment. Waste-land converted into farm land helped the villagers to increase crop production.

Concluding Remarks

This anthropological fieldwork based intervention raised certain key concerns. First, researchers were faced with a conflict of roles during data collection—the role of a researcher versus that of an intervener. Second, researchers faced opposition from a section of social activist group challenging this intervention on the ground that it is not ethical to settle the *Pahari Korwas* on plain as they will lose their identity as so called Primitive Tribal Group. We were viewed as unwanted. To resolve this issue a meeting with social activists, government representatives and anthropologists was organized. The result was positive and we were allowed to carry out intervention work. Informed consent from the Pahari Korwa community was already taken by us.

It raised certain concerns in the context of conducting research and intervention by anthropologists together. In this case, anthropologists were not taken as agent of change but agent of government. It will be relevant to quote Vidyarthi, "Indian anthropologists have faced the challenge to act as social doctors in diagnosing social ills, in prescribing appropriate remedies and smoothing the course of transformation from traditional to transitional stage, and then to the re-organizational phase of our society." (Vidyarthi and Rai 1976: 102-103).

The question of Ethics emerged in this case, whether, anthropologist have exceeded their limits in implementing this project? The general opinion was, they have not but the critics argued that by bringing down the *Pahari Korwas* from their natural habitat to plain settlement was not ethical as it is interference in the natural life of tribal. By settling them on plain the *Pahari Korwa* will lose their present identity as 'Pahari' and be deprived of the facilities by the government in future as so called Primitive Tribal Group. This aspect can only be examined as impact evaluation of the intervention in future

Now, it is placed before the anthropologists to ponder over, whether such initiatives violate the ethics of anthropology or are in the line with acceptable anthropological interventions?

References

Vidyarthi, L.P. and B.K. Rai (1976). *Tribal Culture of India*, Concept Publishing Company, (P) Ltd., Delhi.

Vidyarthi, L.P. (1978). *Rise of Anthropology in India, Vol. II*, Concept Publishing Company, (P) Ltd., Delhi.

CHAPTER 5

Paying Informants in Ethnographic Research

Issues of Ethics and Quality

A.S. ARUNKUMAR AND JESURATHNAM DEVARAPALLI

Introduction

During an interaction with research students, the second author remembered an incident that he happened to come across during his fieldwork among Jenu Kurumba of Masanakudi in the borders of Mudumalai forest. The anthropological course curriculum in India is designed to train the students of anthropology to engage themselves in intensive fieldwork along the community. This gave the opportunity to visit the Jenu Kurumba. Quiet surprisingly, we were astonished by the reception received from the community as we went into the field. We hardly got any response from them on our queries; neglected us in possible ways and found that they were expecting something to satisfy them in return to their response. Maybe this attitude of the tribe is because of being subjected to the constant and repeated research interest by the researchers who forcefully rob their time and the practice of compensating them through gifts or monetary assistance as they turn indifferent.

Many personal anecdotes evoke a major critical issue concerning ethics on research in ethnographic fieldwork in paying or compensating the informants/respondents. Anthropological research adopts the method of ethnography to understand the subject of study. The involvement of pre-industrial tribal communities as research subjects in the ethnographic research in the initial periods of development of anthropology did not demand for any informant consent or did not bother too much on the ethical issues. However, now-a-days the federal agencies insist on high end ethical cautiousness on dealing with human subjects irrespective of subjects. Perhaps, in accordance with the above analogy, this chapter would try to understand the dimensions of paying (including monitory and material) the observed/ informants in the ethnographic study. The chapter would articulate through evolutionary dimensions of ethnography to justify the argument.

Fieldwork Research: An Ethical Remark

Although there is a common consent in general, following ethics in a research, the intensity and different algorithm of ethical dimension that is followed in an experiment research and fieldwork is different. There is a wide difference in the research method and the inter-personal relation between the researcher and the respondents between experimental method and fieldwork method. Anthropology as is well-known is the study of human race encompasses both ways of the research methods for its analysis-the biomedical experimental method and the fieldwork method. As Cassell (1980) describes and analyses the four ideal typical forms of research—Biomedical, Psychological, survey and fieldwork (participant observation), the subject of anthropology fits with the Biomedical and fieldwork method. In whatever form of study the relation between those who is engaged in study and who is being studied tend to change according to the type of study. As Margaret Mead mentions traditionally, those who are studied by experimentation have been called "subjects"; those who are surveyed have been called "respondents"; and those studied by participant observation have been called "informants" (*cf*. Cassell,

1980:29). Cassell in her analysis on the research types with the relationship between the investigator and the respondents adopted four apparent dimensions: (1) the relative power of investigators, as perceived by subjects; (2) the control of the setting where research takes place; (3) the control of the research context—how the interaction is designed and defined; and (4) the direction of research interaction: whether it flows primarily in one direction or two. She found wide contrast between the biomedical and the fieldwork research method. Hence, she concludes that the fieldwork method was more ethically towards the respondent and the biomedical method had the most control with the investigator.

However, the need for ethical refrainment in social sciences arose as a major concern only after the Nuremberg Code, 1966 that emerged as a result of the involuntary consent of the patients to test with new medicines. Perhaps, this lead to critical conclusion of ethical risk involved in the entire research field including the social researches. Ethical review boards strongly recommended the need for a method to incorporate the consent of human subjects to research. It was felt later that mere signature and getting consent alone cannot make the whole thing ethical. And even the increasing tendency of researchers in qualitative research to pay their informants for the research to attract the rate of participation in the research is also to be discussed whether it would fall under the ambit of ethics.

With regards to the ethical stance on paying the informant, there are no proper guidelines among any of the ethical review boards for researches. Instead, the 'ethical guidelines for good practice' laid down in 1987 by the Association of Social Anthropologists of the Commonwealth is that ethnographers should make 'fair return' to respondents for assistance (Srivastava, 1992:17). The term 'fair return' is used instead of 'payment' is to reduce the effect of the return. The guideline, however, does not elaborate on the fairness of return, and the judgment on this is left to the fieldworker.

Classic Ethnography and its Field Relevance on Respondents

Ethnography in the early days was developed by anthropologists through staying in the community; learn their native language and understanding their life processes. In the earlier days, the eagerness of anthropologists to acquire knowledge about the human kind, far about in the remote, inquisitively made them to travel in search of them. The ignorance of native language forced to depend on the sense of eyes rather than the use of ears until the fieldworker learned the native language. Thus, the tool of participant observation gained significant importance in the field of qualitative research. Conducting fieldwork among them; participating in their day to day activities only needed their initial consent of the native people.

A fieldworker's assertive effort and attempt in building up rapport is by constant and repeated self introduction and the ability to gain the belief of the native. Nonetheless, no doubt it depends on the training he had acquired as a fieldworker. Any researcher seeks his rapport through only showing his neutral face; whereby, he attempts to provide any physical, monetary (economic) aid and guidance in difficult situations. This is never considered as a compensation for the local community. However, there are constrains in the fieldwork, the hardship in being in the new alien place and maintaining the local natives is where the success of fieldwork lies as Malinowski in his fieldwork among the Trobriand islanders suffered a lot which is evident from his diary published in 1967 posthumously (Wax, 1972: 9).

Payment in the Field

Informants are very significant in filling the gaps that is created in the process of observations. The relevance of informant is viewed by field researchers in very many ways as to Kauffmen (2002), the informants are not mere informants during his experience of fieldwork rather, they were his overseers. He used the term overseer so to evaluate the recognition of informants in the fieldwork as the informants, many times guides the course of research in the field. In one instance, the researcher was compelled to stay as a tenet in his informant's house and had to rely upon his words until he got a wider rapport with his study people.

There are different ways of representing informants in the literature. One way is to draw a wide line between informant and participant-observer. Informants are defined as local people who willingly provide information to participant-observers. Participant-observers are non-locals involved in intense interaction with members of a community over a long period such as a year or so. The two are not to overlap. In the book on *Nuer*, Evans-Pritchard finds contrasting nature on the approach of two communities on fieldworkers in his fieldwork. He found informants vital to his Azande research and participant-observation central to his Nuer fieldwork. "Azande would not allow me to live as one of themselves; Nuer would not allow me to live otherwise. Among Azande, I was compelled to live outside the community whereas, among Nuer I was compelled to be a member of it" (Evans-Pritchard 1940:15).

Another way of dealing with informants is to minimize their presence. It is widely assumed among ethnographer that participant-observation is superior to relying on informants for data. This is why some fieldworkers require informants to be trained as Evans-Pritchard did, in "dictating texts and giving detailed descriptions and commentaries" (Evans-Pritchard 1940:15). Informants may be uncooperative, they may even lie. But a participant-observer, on the other hand, will note their way of life without hampering the normal course of life of the community. But as a humble learner of it; he has no retainers and intermediaries who obtrude between him and the people, no police, interpreters, or catechists to screen him off from them (Evans-Pritchard, 1962:79).

Information from the field is got through various modes like observation, interacting with the local people, and through documents available. The information got is varied in the process of collection; it can be obtained either from the key informants, other individual or from the community. But when it comes for paying the informants a set of questions arises. Among them, the prior would be to decide upon whether to provide payment to informants or not. And secondly, who should be paid, whether the individual or the community is to be debated.

Impact of Payment/Compensation in Field Research

In a letter to *Man*, Veena Das and J. Parry (1983) asserted the increased tendency of the practice of paying respondents by the contemporary South Asian anthropologists. They claim that practice of paying respondents, the locals, would affect the meagerly-funded, anthropologists, as the hired respondents would be more generous towards their employers. As a consequence, local anthropology will suffer, and so would the prospect of 'mutual critique' (Srivastava, 1992: 18).

Scott G. McNall (1971) pointing the impact of paying the respondent have accorded that the practice will have a negative impact on the overall research perspective. He asserts that it would hamper the relationship between the researcher and the respondents by exploiting the respondents by creating a sympathetic ear instead of a mutual understanding which has to brought out by well-training of the fieldwork by the researcher. Scot feels that it could bias the whole process of research in the field, if the study area is a small and the news of monetary assistance would create a panic situation among the people whereby the whole intention and the character of the respondent is changed as he is coercive and obliged to respond the situation. He further concerns that the graduate students and the future researchers who go for fieldwork on the same field area will feel the suffocation of the payment.

Ethically if the payment to the respondent is legitimized then providing monetary payments for participation can act as an inducement and be exploitative of ethnic community. Alongside the concern for the impact on freely given consent is the concern that paying interviewees might mean they 'tell us what he or she feels we want to know' where the trueness of the response is critiqued. As McKeganey points out, rather than giving an 'authentic' account of their experiences, views and attitudes it may be that the practice of paying research participants is already established and so a 'culture of expectation' that involvement in research will be rewarded financially has been created (McKeganey, 2001: 1237). Moreover, in areas of high spotted points like the tourists spots or hill stations where the native exotic groups are frequently been researched, the attitude of the low wage employers would come to participate in the research process by a few eloquent to get compensation for their response, which would decline the participation of the society at large and these few professional data providers undoubtedly could not effectively represent the society.

The health seeking behaviour of the tribes include a number of practices including the use of plants and animals products (Devarapalli and Kumar, 1998) which they seldom share with their own people. The second author in one of his encounters with Chenchu of Nallamalai forest interested to know what plant and animal products they use for treating different ailments. It has been found to be most difficult to unravel this information from the practitioners in a number of interior settlements. However, in Thummalabailu, a road point village connecting Dornala and Srisaiḷam, the response from the local medicine man is shocking. The moment he came to know the researcher's need he readily came forward to show all the medicinal herbs he uses in their original habitat. Though the response is very encouraging this phenomenal difference is due to the fact that this village is accessible to non-tribal herbal practitioners who come very frequently, engage this man for payment and trivial gifts to collect the herbs. This tendency has led to the depletion of herbs in and around the Chenchu settlement and that may be one of the reasons why the native healers seldom share their knowledge with outsiders so that the species may not be exploited indiscriminately.

The tendency of paying the respondents concerned is however, created by the attitude and urge for information at any cost by the researcher. The inconvenience caused in the field, non-temperament to sustain the difficulties, amateur field experience and lack of training and pressure from the funding agency creates an attitude for paying for the respondents. Payment also renders a fast track data collection procurement so as to complete the project within the time frame. But this kind of commercialization would inflict an amount of damage to the whole process of field based research. However, paying or gifting the respondents in the fieldwork has also got some other good gestures in the research process as it may work as an incentive for further cooperation and moreover it may create a congenial spirit in meeting each other's need provided the commercial angle of it is not project.

Srivastava (1992) in his article 'should anthropologists pay their respondents?' illustrates his own fieldwork experience with the Raikas—the caste of traditional camel-breeders of western Rajasthan in north-west India, from which his instinct of paying the respondents got classified. He argues that the payment to the informants should not be biased within the community. He in his fieldwork finds that his respondent with whom he resided was not in good terms with other members of his community which put the researcher in deep risk in getting unbiased response from the community. Soon the researcher found that the reason for the enmity was—earlier, there was a team of film-makers come to this hamlet and got in touch with the teacher, as he did, for a film which centred around the travel of camel herders of Raikas from their hamlet to the camel fair at Pushkar. So the film crew wanted some herds of camel which the school teacher assured to give along with his brothers and a cousin—who was an ethno-veterinarian of the community without the consent of the community members. All the dealings were negotiated only with the teacher and the traditional and handsome appearance of his cousin fetched an offer to pose an important charter in the film too.

But the secret did not last too long in the small community and the news that teacher and his family benefited by the film crew spread around the community and created disrepute to the teacher's family. The claim for the anger was that the teacher, who was a renowned person in the village, behaved egoistically to earn money and did not inform other community members about the news of need of herds for the film and the remuneration he got from the film-makers.

From the above incident, Srivastava points that in the process of gaining information on this case, two things became clear. First, the people expected a return for their help. Second, returning favours to some but not others were not only jeopardizing amicable relations, it also caused deep, sometimes unbridgeable, cleavages in the local community (Srivastava, 1992: 18). The claim is that when information known to everyone in the community is taken-over by an individual and is rewarded for it and here comes the issue of problem among the community.

But in contrast, the community people were happy with the researchers approach on paying his specialist informants with monetary gift. Because he says, information got from the field may be of two types: specific information and general information. Specific information is information obtained from the specialist like a professional or a patron. And the general information refers to the information that is well-known to most of the individuals present in the community.

A fieldworker in his field, according to Srivastava (1992) has to judge the situation of his presence and the source of obtaining the information. The decision of compensating their respondents is in the interest of the researcher, but one should value constrains of the respondents/the community who accepts the researcher into culture and permits the researcher to intrude into their affairs staying along with them.

The acceptance of ethnography as a powerful tool in understanding the phenomenon, a community, a scenario or an issue with the perspective of holism has provided a credential position in the field of social science research. The emerging adaptability of ethnography to find scope in any of social phenomenon and occurrence is evident in its usage by different researchers for different purpose of research. Ethnography itself has evolved into global ethnography, new ethnography, ethnography of language, multi-site ethnography, multi-species ethnography, ethnography of education, ethnography of law and more and more in the future. The contemporary is not confined itself with the pre-industrial or community based work; rather it has stretched even to urban purview dealing with business ethnography. All these ventures need fieldwork in its complete sense with the availability, accessibility, feasibility and accordance of the respondents. In such cases, research awareness and the notion of time is crucial factor of consideration in the research design.

Conclusion

The trend in which the contemporary ethnographic research is moving, there shall be situation in accordance to which the researcher has to act. The decision of payment of respondent whether it may be of payment in cash of value or gift has to be decided by the researcher. As Srivastava (1992) points out there should be distinction between general and specific informants and compensation can be made as a collective reframe action for the community.

Perhaps, any ethnographic fieldworker who is engaged with a community participating in every aspect of the community life would never let his heart confined to moral and ethical note remembering their cooperation and repaying them in his/her heartfelt way to continue the relationship to post-fieldwork period. But creation of a situation where the respondents make a rightful demand for a negotiated payment would raise the issue of commercialization of ethnographic research leading to many compromises on the quality, quantum and veracity of data. This would in-turn blindfold the researcher in the field as he has successfully strike a business agreement to get the data and this attitude would point out finger on the very integrity of the fieldwork based research which may assume to another dimension of ethics. This entire discourse would unfold the researcher's sincerity and nobility to the research on one side and informant on the other.

References

Cassell, Joan (1980). Ethical Principles for Conducting Fieldwork. *American Anthropologist*. New series, 82(1): 28-41.

Das, Veena and Jonathan Parry (1983). Fieldwork in south Asia. *Man* 18: 790-1

Devarapalli, Jesurathnam and Yathiraj Kumar (1998). Ethnomedicine: The Application of Plant and Animal Products Among Chenchu. *Indian Anthropologist.* 28(2): 73-80

Evans-Pritchard, E.E. (1940). *The Nuer*. Oxford: Oxford University Press.

Evans-Pritchard, E.E. (1962). *Social Anthropology and Other Essays*. New York: Free Press

Kaufmenn, Jeffrey (2002). The Informant as Resolute Overseer. *History of Africa.* 9: 231-255.

McKeganey, N. (2001). To Pay or Not to Pay: Respondents' Motivation for Participating in Research. *Addiction*, 96: 1237-1238.

McNall, Scott G. (1971). On Paying Respondents. *The American Sociologist.* 6 (4):330-331

Srivastava, Vinay K. (1992). Should Anthropologist Pay their Respondents? *Anthropology Today*, 8(6): 16-23.

Wax, L. Murray (1922). Tenting with Malinowski. *American Sociological Review*, 37 (1): 1–13.

CHAPTER 6

Fieldwork for Anthropological Research

Some Ethical Issues

SHYAMAL KUMAR NANDY

Introduction

Fieldwork is synonymous with the anthropological research. It tries to document the variations in terms of biology and culture of the population with the help of certain methods and techniques for generating reliable data. Such data are interpreted and analyzed for academic purpose as well as may be used in the development processes of study population.

Anthropological fieldwork requires a kind of intimate interaction between the anthropological researchers and the subjects chosen for the study. This intimacy generally exists for a limited period of time which is being developed for the purpose of generating data from the field. The professional anthropologists conduct innumerable fieldwork during his life time. Some of the results of fieldwork are published in the form of reports or research papers in academic journals and books. In many cases concerned people do not know regarding the research publication and the contents therein.

Sometimes, the same villages or areas are visited by the anthropologists repeatedly for clearing their ideas regarding established facts and figures or for the purpose restudy in the context of change and transformation. These repeated interventions among the subjects sometimes generate antagonistic attitude towards the anthropological fieldworker because of the fact that the respondents feel exhausted for providing their time and energy without getting anything in return.

In this context, the anthropological fieldwork is becoming complex day by day in comparison to earlier days due to the emergence of a different kind of social situation. New kind of thinking, methods and techniques for anthropological fieldwork are required to cope with the complex situation during anthropological fieldwork.

The nature of anthropological fieldwork has changed over time, since the time of Malinowski and it is still changing due to continuous changes operating in field situations. Malinowski transformed speculative anthropological research of nineteenth-century into a science of society based on deep observation through fieldwork. "The tradition of fieldwork has strongly influenced the content and course of social anthropology. In a way, fieldwork and social anthropology are inseparable. This is perhaps the invisible link that joins contemporary anthropology with what the discipline was in its infancy. Social anthropology is a dynamic discipline, and its practitioners are not ancestor-worshippers. Naturally, it has extended its frontiers, and has witnessed several significant shifts in the foci of its interests. But it remains a holistic discipline and continues to seek its raw materials in fieldwork" (Dube 1978:xv).

The meaning of the word 'fieldwork' is different in different contexts. But, the fieldwork by the anthropologists carries a different meaning. Field is conceived by the anthropologists as a laboratory where experiment is done for gathering experience, scientific experimentation with the facts and figures collected from the field which ultimately contribute to knowledgebase of the human population. Anthropological fieldworker's main objective is to make contact with the people in the villages or towns or elsewhere for gathering different types of information related to human variation in the spheres of biological, cultural and ecological adaptation.

Anthropologists have some unique techniques and strategies to mingle with the people in different field situations for unveiling unknown social and biological facts in which an intimate short term interaction is built up with the purpose of writing something about their social-cultural and biological variations. Professional anthropologists do it according to their needs and write something for their academic interests and publish their observations and interpretations in the academic journals which are disseminated among academic and general people. In the process of anthropological writings we have come to know many unknown social facts. This is the positive side of the anthropological fieldwork.

The fieldwork tradition in anthropological research has evolved to a different kind of exercises coping with the time-frames, manpower, objectives of the contemporary issues at the contemporary social situation with different types of contradictions. Social anthropologists are studying the larger societies other than tribal societies. Earlier traditions of fieldwork are rarely followed by the researchers. Earlier tradition of fieldwork was to gather "the most reliable knowledge of people, societies and cultures is to be had through directly acquainting oneself with them by personal observation, conversing with them in their own language, and living among them and sharing their mode of life for about a year at a time" (Singer 1978: 292). Now-a-days, strategies of fieldwork are different but its basic objective is same.

The mind of the human beings are very delicate to deal with which I have experienced during fieldwork in different research projects as professional researcher. Although good rapport is necessary to encounter in the anthropological fieldwork, still we face some kind of resistance from the field situation in the form of non-cooperation to talk with the researcher. It may be due to lack of time, urgent economic work, some family problems, etc. Such hindrances a researcher may overcome during long stay at the field, but in short span of fieldwork a researcher cannot overcome due to lack of time. In some cases, people are overburdened due to facing so many survey work conducted by panchayat officials as well as researchers visiting the households for very many purposes. Such situations compel them to stay back from the researchers. A good researcher may overcome these types of hindrances during anthropological fieldwork. The researchers are not in a position to compensate the time and energy provided by the general people during fieldwork.

The nature of anthropological fieldwork varies across its sub-disciplines although its basic purpose is same. In Social-cultural anthropology, the researchers mainly depend on the techniques of interview, participant observation and general observation for collection of facts and figures, whereas researchers in the field of Biological anthropology are depending on some specific techniques for collecting blood samples for serological and genetics studies, measurements for growth and nutritional studies, hand prints and toe prints for dermatoglyphics studies, etc. People may talk easily during field investigation but in many cases they are reluctant to offer their blood samples or measurements for academic purposes.

At present, field situation has changed to a great extent. The earlier fieldwork technique for a long period of time is not followed as before due to time constraints and other factors. In long-time fieldwork, a researcher may get sufficient time for mixing up with the people they want to study. But in short-time fieldwork, a researcher may be in a hurry to meet up with time constraints and may exert pressure on the limited available time of the general people which is the causative factor for any kind of resentment during fieldwork.

Fieldwork is a challenging task for the anthropologists due to their involvement with the people in a given social situation. Challenging in the sense that they have to make an inroad in existing social network by dint of their skill of performance either in his own society or otherwise. Involvement means to build up an social atmosphere in which a researcher can swim according to their needs of digging deep into the underlying reality of the social situation without harming the, in any way, existing social order. Any type of anthropological fieldwork should take care of this fact. Otherwise, a researcher cannot make an inroad in the field situation to fulfil their goal to collect data for gathering knowledge of that particular field situation.

Reviews on Anthropological Fieldwork

There are some works on the problems of anthropological fieldwork which are mentioned in this discourse. Srinivas *et al.* (1979) published an edited volume on the problems and challenges in sociological investigation. Most of the papers in this volume highlighted their problems during course of their fieldwork describing their field experiences. Another edited volume was published by A. Beteille and T.N. Madan in the year 1975 entitled as 'Encounter and Experience: Personal Accounts of Fieldwork'. Besides, there are many works related to the ethical issues in anthropological fieldwork (Jarvie 1969; Kloos 1969; Jarvie *et al.* 1963; Clark 1975; Shokeid 1971; Sjoberg 1967).

In the introduction of the book "The Fieldworker and the Field" the editors rightly said that "Success in the field calls for other qualities besides intellectual acumen. The fieldworker should not only tough enough to survive the difficulties and reverses which come his way but have the gift of empathy. He should be able to put himself in the position of individuals from diverse backgrounds, and see the world as they see it" (Srinivas *et al.*, 1979:8).

An edited volume by Surajit Sinha was published by the Indian Anthropological Society based on the seminar on *Anthropological Field Studies on the People of India* in honour of Professor T.C. Das. It deals with various problems in anthropological fieldwork by various authors who have faced during their fieldwork. Two papers in this volume, one by Misra (1978) and another by Roy Burman

(1978), have dealt with the personal ethics in anthropological fieldwork. Misra (1978: 7) mentioned in his paper that "The student of the science of Man becomes the worst exploiter of Man in the sense he even does not bring the finished goods back to the people from whom he took the raw material. He retains it for his own consumption and for the consumption of his like." Roy Burman (1978:116) described his experiences in his paper and stated that "The greatest failure is however that, the investigators who collect massive data in a short time by canvassing long schedules do not get the time or the opportunity to go into the depth of the human situation. They may have a glimpse of the horizon, but they also need to build up their homes in the mind of the people they study. They also need their spiritual fulfilment."

At the end of his paper he also mentioned that "It is not just a question of technique of study; it is a more basic question. I have a search for a home,—if I failed Bhadikara, if Totopara did not contain me,— may be the entire country should be my home. But I have also a trust to help others in my charge to build their homes,—and my great frustration is that I have till now failed in this trust. I wonder how much this failure is structural and how much it is personal" (Roy Burman 1978: 116).

Seshaiah (1979) nicely stated that "Fieldwork means many things to many people. Certainly, a fieldworker's experiences, whether of an emotional or intellectual nature, are bound to be varied depending on the personality of the researcher, his nationality (whether one is studying one's own society or another society matters a good deal), his area or field of research, and on the general as well as individual traits of his respondents."

Field Experience and Feelings in an Anthropological Work

The title of my M.Sc. Part-II dissertation was 'Medical Anthropology of a Tribal Village with Special Reference to the Asur' for which the fieldwork was conducted in the year 1981. My teacher discussed at length various aspects regarding fieldwork with a main focus on health and illness behaviour in a community specific situation and prepared a guideline of field investigation. At that time, it was a feeling of independence for doing fieldwork in an interior place, at the same time, it was a challenge for me to encounter with the people with whom I never faced in my lifetime. I enjoyed the fieldwork as well as natural beauty of Jobhipat village at Netarhat plateau and its surrounding areas. As a student, I faced innumerable difficulties during that fieldwork in terms of field investigation as well as my stay at the *verandah* of the Jobhipat School in the winter season where mosquitoes were abundant. There was no electricity, no latrine, no bathroom, no proper place for defecation, etc. It gave me pain to live in that area for about two weeks. After few days, I adjusted well with the situation, conducted fieldwork, made friendships with the village people and learnt a lot about various aspects of their life situation which I recorded in my note book for the writing of report. I felt that people have an inherent capability to live in any kind of situation with hard labour and with minimum requirements. Initially, I faced the difficulties to communicate with them but overcame with it through learning process of my own. I was totally cut off from my family and friends during that period and my mind was full of joy and happiness to learn the art of anthropological fieldwork. I found out some innovative techniques during data collection which was not taught by my teachers but their suggestions were to try again and again to know the truth or reality. People cooperated immensely with their simple mind, exhausted their time and energy for me. Still, sometimes, I feel that I have got fieldwork experience from them, but I was not in a position to give anything to them.

Concluding Remarks

There are some procedure to make inroads into the field for anthropological fieldwork and the first encounter with the people is important in the sense that it makes some ripples in the existing social order and sometimes love for the researcher and sometimes animosity may come up in the minds of the people which should be judged patiently before making further advancement into the field situation. If some animosity prevails, it is better to take some time to enter into the field. Otherwise, it will not be ethical to make inroads without ignoring people's mind.

References

Beteille, A. and T.N. Madan (Eds.) (1975). *Encounter and Experience: Personal Accounts of Fieldwork*, Delhi: Vikas.

Clarke, M. (1975). Survival in the Field: Implications of Personal Experience in Fieldwork, *Theory and Society* 2:95-124.

Dube, S.C. (1978). Inaugural Address to the Seminar, *In:* Surajit Sinha (Ed.) *Field Studies on the People of India—Methods and Perspectives*, Calcutta: Indian Anthropological Society.

Jarvie, I.C. with P. Kloos and J.A. Barnes (1963). Some Ethical Problems in Modern Fieldwork, *British Journal of Sociology* 14:118-34.

Jarvie, I.C. (1969). The Problem of Ethical Integrity in Participant Observation, *Current Anthropology* 10 (2):505-508.

Kloos, P. (1969). Role Conflicts in Social Fieldwork, *Current Anthropology* 10 (2):505-522.

Misra, P.K. (1978). Anthropological Fieldwork: Some Awkward Questions, *In:* Surajit Sinha (Ed.) *Field Studies on the People of India—Methods and Perspectives*, Calcutta: Indian Anthropological Society.

Roy Burman, B.K. (1978). My Anthropological Field Situation: A Lost Home or a Promised Horizon, *In:* Surajit Sinha (Ed.) *Field Studies on the People of India—Methods and Perspectives*, Calcutta: Indian Anthropological Society.

Seshaiah, S. (1979). Selecting a 'Representative' Village—A Village in Japan, *In:* M.N. Srinivas, A.M. Shah and E.A. Ramaswamy (Eds.) *The Fieldworker and the Field—Problems and Challenges in Sociological Investigation*, Delhi: Oxford University Press.

Shokeid, M. (1971). Fieldwork as Predicament Rather Than Spectacle, *European Journal of Sociology*, 12:111-122.

Singer, M. (1978). Social Anthropology and the Comparative Study of

Civilizations, *In:* Surajit Sinha (Ed.) *Field Studies on the People of India—Methods and Perspectives*, Calcutta: Indian Anthropological Society.

Sjoberg, G. (Ed.) (1967). *Ethics, Politics and Social Research*, Cambridge: Harvard University Press.

Srinivas, M.N. with A.M. Shah and E.A. Ramaswamy (Eds.) (1979). *The Fieldworker and the Field—Problems and Challenges in Sociological Investigation*, Delhi: Oxford University Press.

Chapter 7

Ethical Issues of Anthropology with Special Reference to Fieldwork

Samar Kumar Biswas

Ethics and Ethical Issues in Research

Ethics mean the moral principles that govern a person's behaviour or how an activity is conducted. Ethics mean a set of moral principles. But the morality or ethics vary in society to society, and it depends on their perceptions—what is right or wrong; what ought to be done or ought not to be done; why I should or should not do it. Again, with the passage of time and place, the perception related to ethics or morality of a particular society at a given time and place may be changed. In general, when the behaviour is widely accepted by the society which should bear the values and indicate the perceptions of the society, it is related to morality or ethics. It should be in favour of well-being of the concerned society. Cassell and Jacobs (1987) stated that many anthropologists perceive ethics as an abstract and, on occasion, intimidating set of injunctions. Raymond Baumhart, a sociologist, opined that firstly, ethics refers to well-founded standards of right and wrong that prescribe what human beings ought to do, usually in terms of rights, obligations, benefits to society, fairness, or specific virtues. Secondly, ethics refer to the study and development of one's ethical standards. Though feelings, laws, and social norms can deviate from what is ethical (Baumhart 1968). In this concern, David B. Resnik (2010) stated that, "ethics" is the norms for conducting that distinguish between acceptable and unacceptable behaviour. He also said that, 'ethics' focuses on the disciplines that study standards of conduct, such as philosophy, theology, law, psychology, or sociology. According to him, one may also define ethics as a method, procedure, or perspective for deciding how to act and for analyzing complex problems and issues. In this regard, he used an example, in respect of a complex issue like global warming, while an economist might examine the cost and benefits of various policies related to global warming, an environmental ethicist could examine the ethical values and principles at stake. In this regard, he stated that many different disciplines, institutions, and professions have norms for behaviour that suit their particular aims and goals. These norms also help members of the discipline to coordinate their actions or activities and to establish the public's trust of the discipline. Ethical norms also serve the aims or goals of research and apply to people who conduct scientific research or other scholarly or creative activities (Resnik, 2010).

However, Shah (2006) mentioned that ethical problems arise at various stages of the research: student's enrolment; supervisor's appointment; choice of subject of research; student-supervisor relationship; supervisor's misuse of student's data and ideas; examiners' appointment; examiners' behaviour vis-à-vis student and supervisor; plagiarisation; funding; publication; etc. (Shah, 2006). Apart from these, all research works as well as publications are not up to the mark or mediocre. Even authenticity of data can be questioned as in many cases these are collected by semi-skilled research investigators or researchers. Thus, in many cases interpretation, analysis and report writing are based on lacking of proper information as well as data. With these mediocre research works, the real problems cannot be identified. So, to solve the problems, the recommendation related to this work for policy making should not be expected fully correct. Even sometimes the data as well as reports are misused by the researchers, which may harm the community, thus, the relevance of research may be questioned.

It is true that the researchers face several problems in various stages to conduct their research work. In this context, Resnik (2010) mentioned that there are several reasons why the ethical norms are important to adhere in research.

1. First, **norms promote the aims of research,** such as knowledge, truth, and avoidance of error. For example, prohibitions against fabricating, falsifying, or misrepresenting research data promote the truth and avoid error.
2. Second, ethical standards promote the **values that are essential to collaborative work**, such as trust, accountability, mutual respect, and fairness. For example, many ethical norms in research, such as guidelines for authorship, copyright and patenting policies, data sharing policies, and confidentiality rules in peer review, are designed to protect intellectual property interests while encouraging collaboration. Most researchers want to receive credit for their contributions and do not want to have their ideas stolen or disclosed prematurely.
3. Third, many of the ethical norms help to ensure that researchers can be held **accountable to the public.** For instance, federal policies on research misconduct, conflicts of interest, the human subject's protections, and animal care and use are necessary in order to make sure that researchers who are funded by public money can be held accountable to the public.
4. Fourth, ethical norms in research also help to build **public support** for research. People like to fund research project more if they can trust the quality and integrity of research.

5. Finally, many of the norms of research promote a variety of other important **moral and social values,** such as social responsibility, human rights, animal welfare, compliance with the law, and health and safety. Ethical lapses in research can significantly harm human and animal subjects, students, and the public. For example, a researcher who fabricates data in a clinical trial may harm or even kill patients, and a researcher who fails to abide by regulations and guidelines relating to radiation or biological safety may jeopardize his health and safety or the health and safety of staff and students (Resnik, 2010).

Ethical Issues in Fieldwork in Anthropological Research

In respect to anthropological research, students, scholars and teachers along with the target groups like folk communities of a given society face many problems. The anthropologists collect the first hand data from the field primarily. During collection of information as well as data, report writing they face several ethical problems in most of the times as they deal with the human beings in the field. Even as the researchers do the intensive fieldwork and that is why sometimes they come to know various hidden facts related to indigenous knowledge, particularly the source of ethno medicines, illegal logging, bio-piracy, murder issue, extra-marital relations and so on. In this concern, if deforestation is happened in front of the researchers or medicinal plants are robbed, or a murder is committed in front of researcher or he is informed about the fact, then what should be done by the researcher? Could these facts be documented or reported? However, if the research work does not help the society for any development, has it any relevance? Sometimes, the researcher creates some problems in the research area or field that may hamper further fieldwork. Even the informant or the host may be annoyed to help or say anything to the researcher. The target group often provides wrong information due to researcher-informant subjectivity. They even refuse to provide the data due to misbehave and ask what benefit they are going to get by doing this! They even oppose developmental work as that is not in a sustainable way or rampaging their World View. Issue becomes politico-religious when the community suffer from monopolizing all the resources by mainstream that let them debarred creating a problematic situation. Questions of Human Rights (Indigenous Rights for Indigenous Peoples: ILO) in so many forms as well as Intellectual Property Rights are raised regarding illegal transmission of knowledge and bio-piracy (such as of ethno-medicines and indigenous knowledge). Then what types of ethics should be followed by the researcher? Obviously, these will affect the development of the research as well as subject. In this concern, in the light of ethical point of view some of the important issues, which were faced by the researcher, are being stated below through some examples.

Case 1: Being a teacher of Anthropology, we went to Jalpaiguri district, West Bengal to conduct the departmental fieldwork for M.Sc. first year students on a tribal community. They lived in an extreme remote area with other tribal and non-tribal people. Due to its remoteness we had to face a lot of problems to arrange our accommodation. Somehow we could accommodate our students and ourselves in two different houses at the said village. The people when came to know our background (that we are from Anthropology), suddenly they became astonished and we did not get the proper attention. After three days, we asked one of our hosts about such behaviour. Then he told us that around one year ago one research investigator came from another organization and made an affair with a non-tribal woman who stayed there on account of her job. However, the said research investigator after completion of his research work left the field but did not marry her. After that we tried to convince the host and some of the key informants we had no relation with him at all. Furthermore, he was from another organization and his culture was totally different from us.

Our dilemma: Should we tell it to our friends, colleges, relatives or so on? When questioned by the hosts should we ignore the matter that we did not know him?

Our decision: We did not discuss about this matter further. We concealed this fact from other friends, colleges as well as institutes. We denied the fact having well known the said research investigator and continue our research work.

Case 2: The North Bengal area particularly Jalpaiguri and Darjeeling district was mostly covered by forest (28.75%) in earlier and yet now a certain portion is covered by forests. From time immemorial the people of several ethnic groups depend on forest resources. In this regard medicinal/herbal plant is an important resource on which they depend on for treatment. But it was observed that several non-tribal traders collected the herbal plants etc. from the jungles for the business outside. Even it was happened in front of us also. It was noticed by several tribal people that they were not getting the adequate medicinal plants as the continuous deforestation was going on and further medicinal plants were being pirated by the traders outside. That's why they had to face a lot of problems for pursuing treatment.

Moreover, the medicinal plants or some other resources which were used for curing the diseases by the indigenous people sometimes the researchers bring out in their reports to enrich the research works. Due to this fact, the matter which was secret among the concerned tribal people became disclosed to the traders as well as common people. After knowing the fact, the Multinational Companies or traders tried to collect all the resources for their business as soon as possible.

Our dilemma: When the medicinal plants etc. are uprooted in this way then what should be done by the researchers? If we protest it, our research may not be continued as some of the local people also earned through this way. Should we inform to the administrators or others? Sometimes, through the report of the researchers the names of the valuable plants etc. are disclosed. Is it ethical? The researchers know the names and importance of the plants etc. from the indigenous people. Later, researcher or the Multinational Company may become the owner of this patent. But who will be the real owner of this patent—the concerned indigenous people, researcher or Multinational Company?

Our decision: The medicinal plants etc. are pirated outside and some of the local people were also engaged in this business. But to continue our research work smoothly we were silent and did not protest. In respect to the ownership of the patent related to the medicinal plants etc. of course the concerned people should be the patent owner as they were well-known about the importance of the medicinal plants as it was already practiced in their society. Therefore, no other can be the patent holder.

Case 3: In the districts of North Bengal when we conducted the fieldwork we observed illegal logging and sawing at least in three tribal villages. The villagers including the concerned tribal people were also involved in this work. In this concern, particularly in two tribal villages huge numbers of tribal people maintained their livelihood depending on it. Huge numbers of Teak, Arjuna and some other valuable big trees were cut down everyday. We came to know that the local police administration and forest department were involved in it. Though the local tribal people cut it but the lion share was distributed among the police and forest department. It was observed that at least in two villages more than 100 people were involved in it. We asked the people about this involvement and deforestation. Then they told us that they were not involved in this work and in earlier they had the involvement in other works. But mainly the said traders involved them as labourer with high payment. That's why they left their traditional work and became involved in illegal logging and sawing. They also requested us not to disclose their name and work in the report. Even, they requested us not to shoot such snaps pictures/photos.

Our dilemma: Deforestation was continuously happening in these areas and lot of people earned in this way. If we disclose it then it would hamper their livelihood. Further, our research work might not be continued and even it might be a risk factor of life too. Again, if it is not disclosed, a part of study will be untouched. Then, what should be done by the researchers?

Our decision: To continue our research on the tribal people in the villages of North Bengal we never bring out this matter though the real economic involvement could not be reported. Again, if we disclose the matter in the reports or to the administration, then further works in other villages might be affected. Thus, we stopped to write the episode in the report. In this way we ignored this matter.

Case 4: During my research work I got the information from the villagers and the close kins of the accused that in some cases daughter-in-law was raped by father-in-law and even such illegal activities were prevalent among the close kins also; wife was tortured by her husband and his family members. Even sometimes wife was beaten and killed by them also. However, it was rampant happened in the studied area.

Dilemma: Due to close interaction with the villagers and close kins of the accused, the researchers got the every information related to this above fact. Then what step should be taken by the researcher? Should it be written in the report or disclosed to the others?

Decision: As extra-marital relation as well as rape, illegal affairs within the close kins are strictly prohibited and it is related to the status of the family and society, therefore, if this matter is disclosed then it may affect the status, prestige of the concerned family and society. Even in this way the society may be negatively criticized by the outer world. Thus, the status, good faith may be shaken seriously. In this concern, if the fact is not disclosed, then it would be difficult to understand the problem as well as gravity of work, and which situation forced them to get involved in this type of affairs. I kept concealed their names but disclosed the fact in a general way in report. In case of wife battering, abusing or killing, I used the above conception. As to understand the overall situation and identify the problems it was necessary to me to state the fact without using their original names in the report and even it was not given to the police for investigation.

General Observation and Remarks

Anthropology is a holistic study of mankind with both biological and cultural endowments. Therefore, study on the same biological species in a living condition is rather a very tough job. In this concern to conduct the research work on human beings, teachers, students, researchers, informants, practitioners or folk communities are relativistic and hence become subjected to one another during the research. In cross-cultural study, such scopes of ambiguity and bias are much higher. It is true that the people who are involved in research work face several problems in various stages. The researchers face several problems like behaviour of the students and supervisor, technical problems related to enrolment, publications, funding, and so on.

In this concern, particularly to conduct the research work in Anthropology, the researchers often face several ethical problems which arise at various stages of the research. As the researchers of Anthropology have to do the works on human beings and collect data through intensive fieldwork. This is very sensitive as they deal with the human beings and their culture as well.

During fieldwork, some of the illegal matters like bio-piracy including robbing the medicinal plants, illegal logging, murder and some domestic violence etc. are happened in front of the researchers or even sometimes the researchers could know some illegal affairs. Even misbehave with the informant by the researchers creates serious problems to conduct further study. Often the researchers use the original name of the accused (subject) and state the facts in details in report which sometimes may create various problems as these are deeply related to the status and prestige of the individual and society too. However, if these facts are not written in the report properly then the problems of the concerned people will not be solved. In this concern, the researchers should follow the minimum ethical norms to conduct research work otherwise they may face some troubles. Thus, they should have to know, which information or data will be collected or not; which fact will be reported or not; and how to collect the data or information for the research work. Name of the medicinal plants and its importance, other indigenous knowledge etc. of the concerned people are published, then the question is who will be the owner of this patent? As this knowledge was emerged from the concerned people, thus they deserve their right over this patent. Therefore, the researchers should be aware of the ethical norms related to illegal transmission of knowledge and bio-piracy.

Under these circumstances, what types of ethical norms should be followed? To do a research work in Anthropology there is a need of proper ethical norms as they conduct it on human beings, otherwise the people who are related with this research work and even the research work, publications and so on will be affected seriously. Intensive fieldwork is necessary for social-cultural anthropologists, thus, they should obey and respect the norms, customs, belief, privacy of the concerned people; and should not debar them from any right. As the subject matter is human being, the researchers must have to be very conscious about their own behaviour as if, it may not create problem further to do the research work or it may not have negative impact on the attitudes towards the researcher and subject too.

Some Suggestions

1. In Anthropology, the researchers conduct their research work on human beings, thus, they should respect human dignity, right and autonomy of the concerned people.
2. Sometimes, some hidden aspects of a community life or some specific practices related to culture of the concerned society are well-known by the researchers and not by the common people of the outer world. So, researcher should maintain the secrecy of that society until permission for the same is not granted.
3. The researcher should take the clear consent from the informants, host and so on for the collection of information, data as well as photo snaps and report writing.
4. The researcher should not do such things that the studied people or community is debarred from their resources and rights and face a lot of problems in their daily life.
5. It is very necessary that research work should help the concerned people and society for their development. The benefits of the research work should be distributed among the concerned people.
6. The researcher should have to give and share the right of ownership of indigenous knowledge/ethno-science to them. Again, proper acknowledgement or credit should be given to the studied people.
7. The behaviour of the field-investigators as well as researchers with the studied people at the ground level should be very polite and should never hurt the subject as well as society. Further, they should promise to ensure future access to the field.

References

Baumhart, R. (1968). *An Honest Profit: What Businessmen say about Ethics in Business*. Holt, Rinehart and Winston, New York.

Cassell, Joan and Sue-Ellen Jacobs (Eds.) (1987). *Handbook on Ethical Issues in Anthropology*, Washington DC: American Anthropological Association.

Resnik, D. B. (2010). *What is Ethics in Research and Why is it Important?* Electronic Document, <http://www.niehs.nih.gov/research/resources/bioethics/whatis/> accessed on 25 December 2011.

Shah, A. M. (2006). Ethics in Sociological and Social Anthropological Research: A Brief Note, *eSocialSciences Conference Paper: Ethics in Social Sciences July 2006.*

Chapter 8

Global Ethic, Rights and Responsibility

Madhurima Chowdhury

Introduction

Ethics comprises standards, values and conceptualizations of human purpose that are applied in making judgments about humans ought to do in certain situations. Ethics, also known as moral philosophy, is a branch of philosophy that addresses questions about morality—that is, concepts such as good and evil, right and wrong, virtue and vice, justice and crime, etc. Ethical norms are variously understood as implicit in cultural forms, as grounded in human psychology or as a real component of the world that is discovered by human reason. Global Ethic is nothing but the necessary minimum of common values, standards and basic attitudes. However, anyone who is interested in seeing human rights fully respected and more effectively defended throughout the world must surely also be interested in achieving a change of consciousness concerning human obligations or responsibilities. These need to be seen in the context of global challenges and efforts to establish a global ethic, an ethic for humankind.

Global Ethic and Human Rights

Ethics is therefore often the product of particular traditions of a community, either a particular society, or portion of society, or more widely, it is the product of the particular history of large numbers of societies, allowing us to speak of the ethics of the human community. At this most basic level, ethics, human rights and the developing global interactions of the whole human races are also intimately intertwined. In our hierarchy, human rights seem to occupy an intermediate stage between values and moral foundations and the immediate personal decisions, which concern ethics. In this, they are akin to law, particularly international law, and yet not to be identified simply with law. Many moral controversies today are couched in the language of rights. Indeed, we seem to have witnessed an explosion of appeals to rights—gay rights, prisoners' rights, animal rights, smokers' rights, fetal rights, and employee rights. The appeal to rights has a long tradition. A right is a justified claim on others. For example, if I have a right to freedom, then I have a justified claim to be left alone by others. Turned around, I can say that others have a duty or responsibility to leave me alone. If I have a right to an education, then I have a justified claim to be provided with an education by society. Moral rights are justified by moral standards that most people acknowledge, but which are not necessarily codified in law; these standards have also, however, been interpreted differently by different people.

One of the most important and influential interpretations of moral rights is based on the work of Immanuel Kant, an eighteenth century philosopher. Kant maintained that each of us has a worth or a dignity that must be respected. This dignity makes it wrong for others to abuse us or to use us against our will. Kant expressed this idea in a moral principle: humanity must always be treated as an end, not merely as a means. To treat a person as a mere means is to use a person to advance one's own interest. But to treat a person as an end is to respect that person's dignity by allowing each the freedom to choose for him or herself (Andre and Velasquez 1990).

Kant's principle is often used to justify both a fundamental moral right, the right to freely choose for oneself, and also rights related to this fundamental right. A young person's right to an education, for example, imposes on us a duty to provide that young person with an education. Respecting a right then requires more than merely not acting; rights impose on us the duty to help sustain the welfare of those who are in need of help.

Whenever we are confronted with a moral dilemma, we need to consider whether the action would respect the basic rights of each of the individuals involved. Rights, play a central role in ethics. Attention to rights ensures that the freedom and well-being of each individual will be protected when others threaten that freedom or well-being. If an individual has a moral right, then it is morally wrong to interfere with that right even if large numbers of people would benefit from such interference. But rights should not be the sole consideration in ethical decision-making. Relying exclusively on rights approach to ethics tends to emphasize the individual at the expense of the community. And, while morality does call on us to respect the uniqueness, dignity, and autonomy of each individual, it also invites us to recognize our relatedness—that sense of community, shared values, and the common good which lends itself to an ethics of care, compassion, and concern for others.

Rights and Responsibility

"No rights without responsibilities". We in fact live largely in a society in which individual groups all too often insist on rights against others without recognizing any responsibilities that they themselves have. This is certainly not because of codified human rights as such, but because of certain false developments closely connected with them. In the consciousness of many people these have led to a preponderance of rights over responsibilities. Instead of the culture of human rights which is striven for, there is an often uncultured exaggerated claim to rights which ignores the intentions of human rights. The "weakness of human rights" is in fact not grounded in the concept itself but in the lack of any political and moral will on the part of those responsible for implementing them. To put it plainly: an ethical impulse and a motivation to accept responsibilities are needed for an effective realization of human rights (Dahrendorf, 1990). Many human rights champions active on the fronts of this world who confess their "Yes to a Global Ethic" have already explicitly endorsed that point of view. A Declaration of Human Responsibilities must extend further and begin at a much deeper level. Indeed the two basic principles of the Declaration of Human Responsibilities already offer an ethical orientation of everyday life which is as comprehensive as it is fundamental: the basic demand, "Every human being must be treated humanely" and the Golden Rule, "What you do not wish to be done to yourself, do not do to others" (UDHR, 1948). Certain human responsibilities must be fulfilled first, by individuals or a community, before one can claim human rights. These are given with the human person, but this person is always at the same time one who has rights and responsibilities: Like the Declaration of Human Rights, the Declaration of Human Responsibilities is indeed primarily a moral appeal. A key feature of the Declaration of Human Responsibilities is that it precisely does not aim at legal codification, which is impossible anyway in the case of moral attitudes like truthfulness or fairness. It aims at voluntarily taking responsibility. The Declaration of Human Responsibilities should, therefore, be considered as morally rather than legally binding.

Universal Rights

Efforts to establish a global ethic have received widespread international backing in recent years. Two documents are of particular relevance:

(1) On 4th September 1993, for the first time in the history of religion, delegates to the Parliament of the World's Religions in Chicago adopted a "Declaration toward a Global Ethic."

(2) On 1st September 1997, again for the first time, the Inter Action Council of former presidents and prime ministers called for a global ethic and submitted to the United Nations a proposed "Universal Declaration of Human Responsibilities", designed to underpin, reinforce and supplement human rights from an ethical angle.

The Universal Declaration of Human Responsibilities supports and underpins the Universal Declaration of Human Rights from an ethical angle, as announced in the preamble: "We... renew and reinforce commitments already proclaimed in the Universal Declaration of Human Rights: namely, the full acceptance of the dignity of all people; their inalienable freedom and equality, and their solidarity with one another." If human rights are not being asserted everywhere that they could be, this is usually for want of the necessary political and ethical will. Even the most fervent of human rights activists must acknowledge that "the rule of law and the promotion of human rights depend on the readiness of men and women to act justly." (UDHR 1948)

The Basic Principles are

Article 1

Every human being, regardless of social origin, sex, property, colour, language, nationality or religion, ought to be treated humanely.

Article 2

All human beings should oppose all forms of inhumanity, especially fanaticism, hate, and social exclusion, and work for greater humaneness.

Article 3

No individual human or group of humans, including the state, social class, pressure group, police or military agency stands above the ethical dictates of good and evil. All should behave in a genuinely human fashion, that is: Do good and avoid evil.

Article 4

All human beings, endowed with reason and conscience, should act towards one another in a spirit of sisterhood/brotherhood. Therefore, there should be applied to all human beings, both individuals and groups, including among others families, communities, races, nations, and religions, the long-standing principle of so many ethical and religious traditions: What you do not wish done to yourself, do not do to others.

Article 5

Every human being is always to be treated as an end, never as a mere means, always as a subject of rights, never as a mere object, whether in business, politics, communication, scientific research or other areas of life.

Article 6

No one, except in the case of self-defense, has the right to injure or to kill. Every human being should have respect for life.

Article 7

Although every human person is infinitely precious and must be unconditionally protected, the lives of animals and plants which inhabit this planet with us likewise deserve protection, preservation, and care. That is, we humans are a part of nature, not apart from nature. Hence, as beings with the capacity of foresight we bear a special responsibility—especially with a view to future generations—for the air, water, and soil, that is, for the earth, and even the cosmos.

Article 8

Conflicts ought to be resolved without violence. This principle is valid for all institutions, especially states, as well as for individuals. Particularly public officials are obliged to work within a framework of a just order and to commit themselves, whenever possible, to non-violent, peaceful solutions.

Article 9

No one has the right to rob or dispossess in anyway any person, group of persons, or the commonweal. Every human being ought rather to deal honestly and fairly.

Article 10

Property, limited or large, carries with it an obligation; ownership not only permits the personal use of property but also entails the responsibility to serve the common good.

Article 11

Economic and political power should not be misused as instruments of domination, but for service to humanity. Therefore, mutual respect and the will to mediation should be fostered so as to reach a reasonable balance of interests in a sense of moderation and fairness.

Article 12

Wherever rulers repress the ruled, institutions threaten persons, or might oppresses right, human beings have not only the right but the responsibility to resist—whenever possible non-violently.

Article 13

No one should speak lies. Every human being ought rather to speak and act truthfully.

Article 14

The communications media, to whom the freedom to report for the sake of truth is entrusted and to whom the office of guardian granted, do not stand above ethics but have the obligation to respect human dignity, human rights, and fundamental values. They are duty-bound to objectivity, fairness, and humaneness. Hence, they have no right to intrude into individuals' private spheres, manipulate public opinion, or distort reality.

Article 15

Politicians, scientists and artists are doubly obliged, as individual persons and as society's leaders, to model ethical standards, and especially to serve truth.

Article 16

Religious persons, and especially religious leaders, whose religious freedom is guaranteed, ought to avoid prejudice, fanaticism and hatred towards those of different belief, let alone incite or legitimize religious wars. They rather should always be guides for truthfulness in thinking, speaking, and acting.

Article 17

All individuals and groups are obliged not to treat other persons as mere sex objects or disadvantage them because of their sexuality. Rather, men and women should treat each other in their sexual and kindred relationships with respect and as equal partners.

Article 18

Young people should learn at home, school, religion and elsewhere in society that sexuality in itself is a creative and positive—not a negative, destructive, or exploitative—force. As a life-affirming shaper of community, sexuality can be effective only when partners accept the responsibility of caring for one another's happiness.

Article 19

Marriage, which, despite its cultural and religious variety, should be characterized by love, loyalty, and permanence and guarantee mutual security and support.

Article 20

In the family, parents should not exploit children, nor children parents. Their relationship should reflect mutual respect, appreciation, and concern.

Article 21

The different professions and other societal groupings, such as medicine, business, journalism, among others, should develop current codes of ethics which will relate to the ethical principles of this Declaration by providing more specific guidelines.

Article 22

Nothing in this Declaration may be interpreted as implying for any state, group or person the right to engage in any activity aimed at the destruction of any of the rights, freedoms or responsibilities set forth in the 1948 UN Universal Declaration of Human Rights or subsequent UN documents. (UDHR, 1998)

Concluding Remarks

"All human rights are by definition directly bound up with the duty to respect them". Deile (1997) who is interested in seeing human rights more fully respected and more effectively defended throughout the world must surely also be interested in achieving a change of consciousness concerning human obligations or responsibilities. It would be wrong to think that the legal validity of human rights depends on the actual realization of responsibilities. Human rights cannot be considered as a reward for good human behaviour. The popular use of the concept of human rights has coincided with a growing belief that we are living in a global community, where our interests are closely connected to those of others who may not live in the same state or even on the same continent as us. Precisely in the light of this it becomes clear that human rights and human responsibilities do not mutually restrict each other for society but supplement each other in a fruitful way—and all champions of human rights should recognize this as a reinforcement of their position and their struggle. While ethics, rights and responsibilities can be clearly distinguished, they cannot be separated. The relationship between them must be described in differentiated terms. They are not quantities to be superficially added or subtracted, but are interrelated dimensions of humanity in both the individual and the social sphere.

References

Andre, Claire and Manuel Velasquez (1990). Rights Stuff, *Issues in Ethics* 3 (1).

Dahrendorf, R. (1990). *Reflections on the Revolution in Europe*, London: Chatto Windus.

Deile, V. (1997). Rechte bedingungslos verteidigen, *Die Zeit*, 21 November, 1997.

UDHR (1948). *Universal Declaration of Human Rights*, New York: United Nations.

UDHR (1998). Universal declaration of human responsibilities, *Ethics and International Affairs* 12 (1): 195-199.

Chapter 9

Ethical Issues in Research on Social-Cultural Anthropology

Ashok Das Gupta

Introduction

Ethics mean the moral principles that could be implied to any person, group, association, community, society and its institutions. In research there is also a role of ethics to decide what to do and what not. Suppose, can we clone an individual or enhance illegal organ transfer? So many questions could be raised in social research also. There should be a monitoring committee or agency on the basis of a model code of conduct or certain unanimously accepted measures to see the moral principles are not being violated. We do research with an objective to get accurate result without any error. But in social research, this is not however fully possible. In social research the person has to try minimizing bias and reducing the subjectivity. Researcher has to keep in mind that at the time of research he or she could not react like a policy-maker but doing the duty to collect information in a proper manner. At the same time, researcher would try the best to overcome own perception and not let the target group being much subjective to his/her appearance. However, output of the research should be in favour of well-being of the concerned society. Or otherwise the research seems to be quite meaningless, only of pure type, ideal and less applicable.

"The field of ethics (or moral philosophy) involves systematizing, defending, and recommending concepts of right and wrong behaviour. Philosophers today usually divide ethical theories into three general subject areas: metaethics, normative ethics, and applied ethics. ***Metaethics*** investigate where our ethical principles come from, and what they mean. Are they merely social inventions? Do they involve more than expressions of our individual emotions? Metaethical answers to these questions focus on the issues of universal truths, the will of God, the role of reason in ethical judgments, and the meaning of ethical terms themselves. ***Normative ethics*** takes on a more practical task, which is to arrive at moral standards that regulate right and wrong conduct. This may involve articulating the good habits that we should acquire, the duties that we should follow, or the consequences of our behaviour on others. Finally, applied ethics involves examining specific controversial issues, such as abortion, infanticide, animal rights, environmental concerns, homosexuality, capital punishment, or nuclear war" (Fieser, 2009).

Ethics in Anthropology

Ethics in anthropology is an emerging issue. We have so many theories and methodologies in accordance to which we can promote our study. Again, the group of people or the subjected group is with its social, economic, political and religious criteria that begin with mode of production on the basis of resource available and supported by cultural values. Each and every community has its own educational system and health related practices. And there is always a question of ethnocentrism. Anthropologists are trying to be relativistic to overcome biases during doing research on living being. Anthropologists are trying to postulate certain codes of ethics and from time to time they modify the same. They have to think about how much they can disclose their experiences to the public. Many things are definitely to be learnt from the alternatives, but we have the duty to protect them also, at least ensure that there would be no harm from our side during conducting the research or while disclosing the documentations. And anthropologists can also contribute in understanding the alternative or native or the indigenous or folk and common people and that could help in promoting modern input, sustainable development and progress in the society. May their contribution be a little, but till then they could contribute a lot. After all, anthropologists have to deal with human with humanity. And that is the ethics in anthropology. Anthropological research should be ethical. Actually, ethics should be there in not only with the understudied groups, but also with the public, the discipline, the students, the sponsors, and to one's own government and to host governments. However, that would be a greater issue to discuss in. Here in this chapter, the focus has been primarily on the research. We have to look after whether the group is pre-agriculturist, agriculturist or post-agriculturist; its division of labour that is the social system; its economy and polity, religious belief, health system, educational institutions, mind-set and culture. Only then we could do a good research in a systematic way.

American school of anthropology emphasizes more on cultural perspective of folk life that puts more emphasis on value system of an indigenous or an aboriginal or a native society or community or a section or group of people; their mode of production on the basis of available natural resources holds their overall concept of feedback, division of labour, institutions and organizations. Researcher and informant from the reference group generally possess different value systems. So, issue of cultural relativism appears. There has been always a try to overcome the errors in anthropological research due to more subjectivity and researcher-informant bias. We can see it as a clash between the modern and traditional perceptions. And in post-colonial era, researchers could not remain so much biased towards the people living beyond modernity and those who have to be brought under the modernity. Modernity has some drawbacks within it and perhaps information from traditional way of living can facilitate in filling up the blanks. Even services from the traditional domains can reach up to the global standard. Some of the basic problems out of modernity are global warming and pollution, unidirectional development and the question of sustainability, loss of biodiversity and the issue of resource management, genetic engineering and emergence of resistant varieties of pathogens, politico-economic problems and their shadow on socio-religious aspects, and drastic changes in health and educational system with both good and bad motives when people are on a way towards informal to formal sector. Being a democratic organization, American Anthropological Association (AAA, founded in 1902) was the first to postulate ethics in anthropological research. AAA has worked so far upon the concept of racism, incorporation of the subject in school syllabus, preservation of archaeological artifacts at places where big developmental programmes are going on (such as mining and dam construction), and so far. The organization was aware of discriminations and discriminatory laws, obstacles in front of conducting the research, World Wars, nuclear power, Third World Countries, Cold War, developing and underdeveloped countries, and various civil wars and wars and war-like situations. Anthropology can be used by army and intelligence. That might be Vietnam War, secret research in Thailand and Latin America, Near East and Iran. AAA is in favour of protecting the endangered primates. It wants to give protection to the native communities and their culture. It is against any ban towards gay marriage. American Anthropological Association (AAA) in its Code of Ethics of 1971 has emphasized on Relations with those studied, Responsibility to the public, Responsibility to the discipline, Responsibility to students, Responsibility to sponsors, and Responsibilities to one's own government and to host governments.

Anthropologists are bound to protect their physical, social, and psychological welfare; to honour their dignity and privacy; to safeguard their rights, interests, and sensitivities; to conduct the study if only permitted by the understudied group; to communicate the anticipated result of the study to them; to preserve anonymity (in special case, such anonymity may be compromised unintentionally) or use pseudonyms; to incorporate them in research projects; to recognize their social and cultural pluralism as well as plurality of values, interests and demands in those societies in order to overcome irresponsible decisions. Statement on Problems of Anthropological Research and Ethics (1967) and Resolution on Freedom of Publication (1948) were previously postulated by the council of American Anthropological Association (AAA, 1971, 1986).

Like AAA, other important organizations are European Association of Social Anthropologists (EASA), International Union of Anthropological and Ethnological Sciences (IUAES), Association of Social Anthropologists of UK and Commonwealth (ASA) and so forth. These organizations have realized that there is a need of anthropological ethics. Actually, this is required in each state and every country. It has to be implemented internationally also, especially at this very moment of globalization. Anthropologists should have a responsibility towards the nation, but how can they go against the humanity and the other people as a whole. They deal with personal information of persons from the indigenous or the non-Western people; and for sure know-how far discloser of all the information to the public would be against the moral ethics and create a platform of untrust between researcher and informant. Anthropologists have to think about the basic human rights as they are dealing with human beings. For example, indigenous communities hold indigenous knowledge, indigenous culture and indigenous knowledge system which should be provided with some protective measures. All the indigenous communities grouped under the category of Indigenous Peoples are provided with the Indigenous Rights postulated by International Labour Organization (ILO). They should be brought under Intellectual Property Rights because of their intimate understanding of nature and bio-diversity, generation-wise accumulation of information on the basis of trial and error as well as informal experiments. However, secret research should not be revealed to sponsors, public and even the target groups. In case of India, while doing research in social-cultural anthropological research, we should be aware of our polity, economy and socio-religious issues.

Then come out other aspects regarding concealing or revealing of the data, especially when it is too much sensitive and contains personal information. Secret research is also done by anthropologists or other people using anthropological methods. In a country, there is a system of law. In a community, there is a basic frame of norms, values and customs. Sponsors are different. Host country or the research foundation can interfere in the research. The issue is not only confined within researcher-informant or teacher-scholar relationship. Researcher has some responsibility to the public as he or she could not work like a robot. Public on the other side has political, economic, social and religious-cultural perceptions depending on mode(s) of production and division(s) of labour. The nation or country has also a constitution and a foreign researcher could perhaps conduct his/her research as per doing in own country. Again, the research may be of pure or applied or action type. The result may not just for documentation, but it can be applied to a targeted group for certain reasons. Or the research could be conducted in a running situation and subsequently, information of both open and hidden type coming outside could exert a decisive impact over the entire situation. That may be on war, terrorism, abortion, drug abuse, massacre, nuclear programme, political conspiracy, civil war, instances of human right violation, illegal technology transfer, bio-piracy, riots, emigration, manmade disasters, illegal activities, state oppression, gender and other sensitive issues, developmental issues, agenda of sustainability, urbanization, globalization, global market economy, global polity, their impacts on national and local levels. Anthropology is a multidisciplinary subject—it can be related to nearly every discipline under humanities and to a great extent to human science. Policy-makers, government and intelligence can get a benefit of this subject. But there is a chance of misuse and at that point, awareness is a timely approach. Anthropology should serve humanity with a post-structural view (proper documentation) where it can freely analyze the symbols and study on worldview of the targeted population in a more accurate manner. Researcher cannot conduct the study from his or her mind structure and try to overcome the bias when tradition meets modernity or *vice versa*.

In 2009, AAA has approved a new code that classified research is not allowed in certain conditions (AAA, 2009). Anthropology should not be in counterinsurgency or ethnic violation. But in reality we can see that various eminent personalities, film-makers, travellers, NGOs and Civil Society are actively taking part as a mediator in such incidents besides the government, police and administration, Para-military forces and army, and international organizations. Anthropology could be here politically used and misused. But, if anthropologists have some information related to the fruitful solution of the ethnic clash, why not they come out on their own and serve the humanity? That would glorify the subject and people would be more attracted to the subject. Anthropology could clarify itself being the holistic study of mankind. It can deal with sustainability in developmental programmes, express peoples' aspiration, portray a multicultural society and ensure global public services from the other people living close to the nature. So, there should be some liabilities. Models are needed to formulate from various disciplines of humanities that could help us to know the situation and establish proper researcher-informant and teacher-student relation. We are talking about post-structuralism and post-modernity. But, we always need some models that could deliver all or maximum answers to the questions abruptly emerged in the mind of the students, the informants and the researcher-cum-teacher. Exchange of information through regular seminars, symposium and workshops has become eventual. Both qualitative and quantitative methodologies are now being applied. Rapport establishment and impression management are the must at any research programme. Rapid Rural Appraisal and Participatory Rural Appraisal (RRA and PRA) are two crucial methodologies in such in-depth research programmes. Semi-structured schedule based survey, interview, group discussion, focused group discussion, genealogical data, case studies, key-informant's interview, life histories, story narration, observation, analysis of symbols, proper report writing, focus of folk life from both native oriented and science oriented approaches are exclusive here. Study would initiate with a pilot fieldwork and with the help of secondary literature, researcher has to realize the research gap, aims and objectives, formulate research questions, diagnose the situation and give rise to a hypothesis that seems to be the most believed in the religious laboratory of survival and under the category of ethno-science which is still to be justified and proved. There comes the major fieldwork that may be an ethnographic work or a cross-cultural study. If the variables are taken on the basis of available natural resources, micro-environments, biodiversity and ecosystem, we would get the mode of production. This would provide us information related to division of labour. From there we can get the politico-economic and socio-religious information. In this way, we would get structure of the society and its blue-print within the informant's mind (worldview) that would further disclose hidden information traits.

And again, a research work may be wonderful, but at that moment the authority may not permit it for publication. These things are also not beyond ethics. In such cases, the researcher may face so many challenges and even get a mental trauma or he/she could try to move to another institute or research foundation. Because every institution has some opportunities and at the same time obligations. That is a hard reality and no body could deny from that. Fund allotment often decides the extension of fieldwork and sample size. Non-cooperation among the researchers in the same project can put the worst impact on our result and there might be delay in the due process. Often researcher is not supposed to reveal the names of informants, key-informants and case-studies; but has to do so under the pressure of higher authorities. Researcher after hard fieldwork and conducting the research ethically and thoughtfully cannot get much data or find a negative hypothesis. The research work may be based on assumption and philosophical aspects and far from reality. That may be due to the fact that during research not all but a few parameters were being taken into account:

1. Other sensitive issues can be categorically pointed out as a try to change the genes and the process of protein syntheses, genetic engineering, feeding of biotechnologically modified foods, food poisoning, replacement of natural varieties (both domesticated and wild), biodiversity loss, hamper to ecology, natural hazards and global warming. This will hamper the relationship between human and nature. Or we would say that modes of production and reproduction could be heavily affected.
2. Ethics is also involved in body organ transplantation, wrong tissue grafting, eugenics, assertive mating and expression of lethal alleles, natural selection or de-selection, wrong treatment in a given medical system, using bio-chemical weapons, damage to the nervous system and other body organs, and so forth.
3. There might be hampering to mega-structures of a civilization, artifacts on technology, material apparatus of a culture, etc.
4. Cutting of human access to ecological resources, migration and emigration to different ecosystem and climate exert effect on human-nature relationship. A community can loose its modes of production fit to its mode of reproduction.

That can hamper its division of labour and also the social institutions and organizations of its social system.

5. Ethics could be discussed on the basis of formal and informal ways of communications, delivering misinformation, not informing a fact, hiding a fact, corrosion of the fact as well as whitewash of the fact. So, the researcher has to be careful and sincere about the information so far gathered.
6. Change in the modes of message exchange (via language) can hamper human to human interaction. A new language would bring in new thoughts and World View. It is followed by boycott and isolation of the native groups that become marginalized. This is highly empirical, cultural and cognitive.
7. Change in the modes of women exchange such as marriage system can lead to emergence of new sub-structures either positive or negative to the present form of social system. This is actually social. We can add this to the gender issue also.
8. Change in the modes of goods exchange is also crucial. It will decide the fate of economy and polity. We do not know whether the community appreciates barter and traditional economy considering human resource and gold and cattle and agricultural production as the capital. We can not know whether the community says yes to pure economy, rationality, currency system, equity and credit followed by acceptation of modern modes of economy: mixed, macro, micro, micro-financing, and global economy regulated by the market or nationalized bank or the political institution.
9. Human is bound to norms and values, timely and untimely performances, symbols and logic, religious laboratory of survival and successively entire religious organization. These things actually provide support to the best nature-human and human-human relationships in a fixed ecosystem. For a folk community, the religious life and

culture-book (Grey Literature?) deeply embedded within folk cognition (Grey Matter?) are still prominent. There people still relay on sound to song; sign to art and script; as well as gesture to personality. This we can say Human-Supernature relationship. With modernity, religious and magical systems are examined by science and medical practices.

10. We can see the whole politico-economic domain as well as socio-religious aspect from local, national and international perspectives.
11. Ethics is associated to Human-Nature, Human-Human and Human-Supernature interactions. We can see this through Nature-Human-Supernature or artifact-sociofact-mentifact interlinks. Many describe this in the way of Substructure, Structure and Superstructure.

Concluding Remarks

First of all researcher has to be humanitarian with a wider point of view and least bias that depends on the person and not any training course or declaration. Social researchers like anthropologists have to respect the other and show a notion of responsibility. Establishment of a committee for social-cultural anthropological research to me is much harder than any science subject including physical anthropology that would merely highlight on teacher, scholar, students subject group, institution, agency, authenticity and application of the work.

Culture as an unwritten book preserves the entire message regarding political and religious organizations as well as economic and social institutions. So, study of culture at micro-level is very necessary, which is the main objective of social anthropology. Personally as a researcher in Social Cultural anthropology, I strongly believe that Culture is just like a unwritten book that decides the economic and social institutions motivated by political and religious institutions: the study in anthropology is very sensitive to bias, so it is moral duty of the researcher to try level best in order to avoid biasness during communication and other interactions; we have to reduce the scope of subjectivity and increase objectivity. We have to be very careful about research approaches, methods, methodologies and ethics.

References

American Anthropological Association 1971 (1986). *Statements on Ethics—Principles of Professional Responsibility.* Electronic Document <http://www.aaanet.org/ stmts/ ethstmnt.htm> Accessed on 10th November 2011

American Anthropological Association, (2009). *Code of Ethics of the American Anthropological Association.* Electronic Document <http://www.aaanet.org/ issues/policy-advocacy/Code-of-Ethics.cfm> Accessed on 10th November 2011

Fieser, J. 2009 (2003). *Ethics.* University of Tennessee at Martin. Internet Encyclopaedia of Philosophy (IEP): A peer-reviewed academic Resource. Electronic Document <http://www.iep.utm.edu/ethics/> Accessed on10th November 2011

Chapter 10

Ethical Issues in Epidemiological Study of Type 2 Diabetes among the Gangadikara Vokkaliga of Karnataka State

S. Yaseen Saheb, D. Xaviour, B.V. Raviprasad, Md. Salman, S. Dasgupta, M.A. Shekar, H. Basavana Gowdappa, K. Raghothama Rao, D. Ravindranath, P.B.S.V. Padmanabham, B.N. Sarkar, D. Lokanath and S. Samanta

The Human Genome project has opened new fields of research in Epidemiology, Human Genetics and Genomics. This lead to several ethical issues in utilizing the human biological samples, widely debated in public domain. Several countries formulated ethical guidelines in conducting biomedical research. In tune with this, Indian Council of Medical Research (ICMR) revised guidelines for biomedical research on human participants in the year 2006.

The Anthropological Survey of India launched the epidemiological study of type 2 diabetes among the Gangadikara Vokkaliga of Karnataka state with an objective to assess the bio cultural risk factors on type 2 diabetes. In executing this project, we adhered to the ethical guidelines stipulated by ICMR. Informed consent of all the participants in the study was obtained after due deliberations with the participants regarding the scope and aims of the study and its usefulness. Slightly deviating from the traditional anthropological fieldwork, we enrolled the participants and invited them to participate in this study. We established Family Diabetic

Research Centre with clinical facilities. Physician, laboratory technician and Phlebotomist were appointed to generate the clinical profiles of participants and to draw human blood samples. Biological Anthropologists have drawn the extended pedigree of the participant. In this chapter, we elucidate how we adhered to the ethical guidelines propounded by the ICMR in drawing human biological samples. We generated 1300 samples of Gangadikara Vokkaliga residing in neighbouring districts of Mysore.

In the past, the physical/biological anthropologist undertook field expeditions in tribal areas and collected blood for serological investigations for several projects since 1950. Human blood was drawn in the field and analyzed in the field situation by establishing a field laboratory. So, the questions of preservation of blood samples for future studies were not contemplated. The researchers managed to convince the people by establishing good rapport, to donate blood samples for such studies with co-operation of the local officials and tribal chiefs. For all the serological studies blood samples were collected by pricking finger tips of the people, but venous blood was never collected in large quantities (10 to 20 ml). The need to obtain informed consent of the participant was not necessitated during the earlier fieldworks.

Anthropological Survey of India established DNA laboratory in tune with Human Genome Project with an objective to screen Primitive tribal groups to trace past human migration routes and to store their DNA for posterity. Several scholars were sent to premier institutes to get trained in art of DNA technologies. As a result, proposals were sent to government for funding to establish DNA laboratories; the first such laboratory was established at Central Regional Centre, Nagpur. Simultaneously, several researchers were deployed to collect blood samples from different locations of the country.

With advent of modern biotechnologies, international agencies overseeing the biomedical research stipulated guidelines to safeguard the interests of the indigenous people and to protect the human rights from being exploited by the multinational companies. In this context, the national governments formulated bio-ethical guidelines for carrying out research on human participants to protect interest of the people. WHO and UNESCO coordinated different agencies and academic bodies in arriving at a consensus in implementing biomedical research involving human participants. One of the criteria laid down was to obtain informed consent of the participant by imparting education regarding the utility of the biomedical research and the benefits that accrue to the society by the research findings.

During the 10th and 11th Five Year Plan period Anthropological Survey of India launched several projects such as DNA polymorphisms in contemporary Indian populations; DNA polymorphisms and diseases; Community Genetics and health; People of India: Bio-cultural adaptations; Genetics, health and Family study. All these studies involved peoples' participation from different eco-cultural zones of the country with varied cultural ethos, where the researchers need to be sensitive to the native cultures while interacting with people in their academic pursuit. To cope with these situations researchers were guided by the ethical norms. All the projects launched by Anthropological Survey of India were multi-disciplinary in nature involving large quantity of biological samples combined with prolonged laboratory analysis in arriving at definite conclusions, thereby necessitating banking and storage of the samples. The complexities involved in the above process forced the authorities to adopt ethical guidelines during the course of the research.

Mysore Family Diabetes study on Gangadikara Vokkaliaga community of Karnataka was initiated by a consortium of institutions: Anthropological Survey of India; Apoorva Diabetes Foundation, Mysore; JSS Medical College and Hospital, Mysore; and South-West Foundation for Bio-medical Research, Texas, USA involving Physicians, Endocrinologists, Biological Anthropologists, Biochemists, Nutritionists and Psychologists. The clinical records available at Apoorva Diabetes Foundation, Mysore, and JSS Medical College and Hospital, Mysore were screened to identify Diabetic patients belonging to GangadikaraVokkaliaga community of Karnataka. Enquiries were made to willing patients to participate in the study and educated them regarding the aims, objective and goals of the study through the Physicians and Endocrinologists. A brochure was prepared in English and Kannada language covering all aspects of the study to give wide publicity to attract people to participate in huge numbers. Extended pedigrees of the Diabetic patients were drawn to enroll them and informed consents forms were obtained after informing about the goals and benefits of the study.

A hospital/clinical environment was created by establishing a counselling centre, blood collection centre, physical examination and laboratory. A wheel chair was made available to the physically challenged and aged people. Two beds were provided for the convenience of the patients. As patients are required to stay for duration of 3 hours for clinical evaluation, seating arrangement with TV facility was provided. Separate toilet facilities for men and women were arranged.

A physician was appointed to generate clinical profile of the participants. A Phlebotomist was recruited to draw venous blood of 10 ml of each participant, both fasting and postprandial. Each non-diabetic participant was administered 75 grams of glucose to measure oral glucose tolerance test. Urine samples (30 ml) were collected from each participant. A laboratory technician was appointed to process biological samples for laboratory analysis.

Each participant was contacted by telephone prior to his/her visit to the laboratory and advised to bring all relatives during early hours of the day for drawing fasting blood. Local transport was arranged for all the participants. Outstation participants were reimbursed bus fares from the place of their residence to FDRC and back. All participants were given refreshments after drawing postprandial blood sample. Each enrolled participant was given an identity card with particulars of name, age, sex, address and specific ID number. Each enrolled participant is expected to visit at least thrice to FDRC. Each enrolled participant was given compensation for the inconvenience and time spent at FDRC as per approved government rates.

All the participants were given the tentative results of the biochemical tests. After examining results, the Physician imparts counselling to the patients.

A personnel file was opened for each participant containing all clinical information, medical history, demographic details, extended pedigrees and results of bio-chemical tests. These files are accessible to only authorized researchers apart from the participant on request.

Reference

Indian Council of Medical Research (2006). *Ethical Guidelines for Biomedical Research on Human Participants*, New Delhi: ICMR.

Index